WHEN GOD WAS BLACK

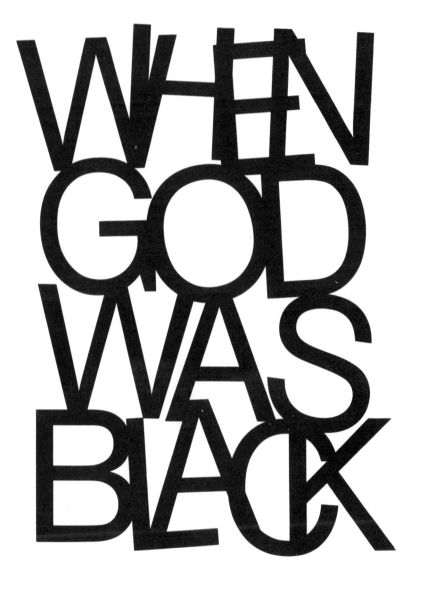

WHEN GOD WAS BLACK

by
BOB HARRISON
with
JIM MONTGOMERY

ZONDERVAN PUBLISHING HOUSE
GRAND RAPIDS, MICHIGAN

CONTENTS

WHEN GOD WAS BLACK

CHAPTER ONE

When God Was Black

Not too long after our Lord's ascension, an Ethiopian believed on Jesus Christ and was baptized.

And God became black.

In the nineteenth century white missionaries went to parts of Africa knowing that their life expectancy was only a few months. They came and they died and many Africans put their trust in Jesus Christ.

And again God was black.

In a rough-hewn, crowded shack in America, a black slave, having nothing in this life but hopelessness and chronic, bone-weary fatigue, found his release in Jesus Christ. From being a miserable slave he became the child of a King.

As the Scripture had promised, the lowly slave was filled with the Spirit of God. God took up His residence in the black slave. The black body became the temple for the Holy Spirit of God. God's exterior was black.

So God was not only white. Or brown or yellow or red.

God was black as well.

In the segregated streets of the South, in the ghettos of Watts and Hough and Newark and Detroit, and in a few — a very, very few — wealthy and influential homes, wherever Jesus has found a home in the heart of our Negro citizens, God is black.

What's it like when God is black?

Are the prejudices swept away, the doors flung open, the awesome power of God just as effective?

I think I can tell you. Because I am black and God lives within me, too.

I'd like to tell you my story of what it's like when God is black.

CHAPTER TWO

The Walls Come Tumblin' Down

I also happen to be a musician. So occasionally I'm asked to sing the spiritual about Joshua and the walls of Jericho.

It's not hard to sing this number with "soul." The song always reminds me that walls have come tumblin' down in my life, too.

Economic walls, social walls, walls of ministry for Jesus, and yes, walls of my own making. Walls of frustration and hatred and prejudice.

Don't think that these walls just disintegrated. The battle scars are there.

And it has not always been a boost to my ego when "Jericho" has been requested. Sometimes facial expressions in the audience say this: "Isn't that a picture? That cute little darkie singing a Negro spiritual."

But the walls *have* come crashing down.

By now I've sung and preached on every continent. I've rubbed shoulders with, I've prayed with, I've ministered with the great and near-great of the evangelical world.

11

I've gone where no other or few other evangelicals of my race have gone. The walls — that have kept most Christian blacks from evangelical schools, pulpits, camps, mission societies, Christian organizations and other places automatically open to those of white skin — have all broken down for me.

Along the way I've frequently been told, "Bob, it would be all right if all the blacks were just like you."

I know this is meant as a compliment, and I accept it as such. But no black appreciates such a remark. I know I don't. Every time, it hurts. It cuts to the bone. It grieves me deeply.

For I know that I have made it only because by the grace of God I have many things going for me.

There's that musical talent. I've also been a college athlete. The Lord has given me an outgoing personality as well as extraordinary physical energy and drive and perseverance. And most of all, I was brought up in a godly, loving home that protected me from many traumas which others of my race have suffered.

So what my well-meaning white Christian brothers are really saying is this: "Bob, we would accept all Christian blacks in our churches if they were all extremely gifted and personable and free from the scars that have marred their childhood and youth. But because most black Christians are the product of their environment (as of course most whites are, too), we don't want them in our churches and in our pulpits and in our schools."

This hurts me because I can't leave behind my many friends and relatives who haven't had the same advantages that I have enjoyed.

If I am accepted only because I am a triple threat, as it were, and my friends and loved ones are left behind because they are quite ordinary, in reality I'm still not accepted either.

The walls have come tumblin' down for me, for which I can only praise God. But for hundreds of thousands — even millions — of my fellow black American Christians, the walls are still there.

For them, when God is black, God is Jim Crowed into a corner.

As I write this, I want to make it plain that I'm not just talking about integration in our churches. It might be that in some places integrated congregations would be useful and helpful and a wonderful testimony to the power of Jesus Christ. In other places, such integration might be completely pointless.

What the black wants is to feel that his place of worship is not being dictated to him. He wants to feel that he can enter any church he chooses, black or white.

But integrating congregations is relatively beside the point.

What is really significant is that millions of black Christians in this country represent a vast potential for the cause of Christ.

Here is a host of believers who can have a vital and significant part in the evangelization not only of the blacks and whites of America but also of a great throng of people around the world.

More and more, it is becoming a disadvantage to be a white-skinned American overseas. More and more, a black exterior is a passport to effective ministry among the world's two billion non-white peoples.

This potential has been largely untapped, primarily because the color of the skin of these American Christians has kept them from the places and the organizations and the experiences whereby they could learn and grow and mature into effective witnesses and servants for Jesus Christ.

When God the Holy Spirit is black, He is quenched.

The black Christian (with token exceptions) is told by the white believer:

"You can't study the Bible in our schools."

"You can't go to the camps where white kids are challenged to give their hearts to Christ, to enter the ministry, and to go to the mission fields of the world."

"And certainly, Holy Spirit-with-a-black-surface, you can't minister and teach and preach outside of your ghettos."

When God the Holy Spirit is black, He is accordingly grieved.

So I am writing this book in the first place to white Christians so that they might understand what they can do to take advantage of this potential. So that they can understand what has been denied the Negro Christian and why so far he has been unable to take his place alongside his white brother in the great cause of fulfilling our Lord's commission to us all. So that they can see wherein they are sinning and thereby grieving and quenching God who dwells in the black man.

I am also writing to my black brothers in Christ.

Why do we cry over discrimination and poverty and blackness?

Why do we grieve and quench the Holy Spirit by our self-pity and self-deception and even by our unconcern and laziness?

God lives in us, too.

God *is* black.

I'm black, too.

So I hope and pray that this encounter with my own crushing defeats and ultimate victories — and the account of my own struggles to let God live through me — will wake us all up.

Blacks *and* whites.

There's a big world out there hungering to know Jesus Christ.

Let's allow God to use all the forces He has available.

Let's quit believing that God is second rate when He is black.

CHAPTER THREE

Who Would Room With a Negro?

Just to show you how naive I was, I was over twenty years old before I realized it made any difference among Christians that I was black.

I don't mean in the secular sense, of course. When I was a lad growing up in San Francisco's Fillmore district the ghettos were just forming. Things weren't as bad there as they were in some other places.

But I wasn't ignorant of what was going on in the South. The news accounts of lynchings, joblessness, Jim Crow laws and later such episodes as that of Emmit Till gave me a hatred for any person from the South.

If I just heard someone speaking with a Southern accent I immediately hated him.

It was the walls of prejudice in evangelical circles which really threw me when I finally encountered them. I didn't know they existed.

I guess it was my church and my family that had sheltered me. If it ever occurred to our church members that racial background made any difference, they never let on.

Every Sunday, rain — and there was plenty of it in

San Francisco — or shine, fog or wind, my family walked the fourteen blocks to Sunday school and church. We sang and praised the Lord and clapped our hands with other Negroes, Japanese, Chinese, Scandinavians and a sprinkling of Filipinos and Mexicans. In those early forties, San Francisco had become the gateway for the Orient and the Mecca for minority groups seeking wartime employment — and our church showed it.

My parents, especially my father, were certainly aware of and had personally experienced many of the racial problems in the world. But they had always taught me that such discrimination did not exist in Christian circles.

"Christians are Christians above everything else," they said.

I came to feel (even though I had not accepted the Lord myself) that being a Christian automatically overcame any barrier. Christian ties were stronger than racial ties, I believed, and would help one to overcome social problems and economic barriers.

I have proved this to be true a thousand times over in the days since my youth, but at that time I was terribly green when it came to the huge dark side of Christianity where racial prejudice was still a way of life.

The result was that when, in my early twenties, I blundered up against my first great wall of prejudice, it shook me and all but destroyed me.

I was ready to throw Christianity out the window, to wipe all whites off the record.

As I look back now, I can appreciate and understand the mentality of the present-day black militants. I was crushed and enraged and ready to lash out in any way to get back at the injustice I felt had been done to me.

The first hint of a problem came as I began thinking about going to a Christian school.

Black Christians at that time, and for the most part up to this moment, were almost completely unaware of the things so familiar to the white Christians. We knew little about Christian conferences, about foreign missions, about white Christian organizations, about evangelical leaders or about Christian schools.

The Youth for Christ meetings which came to San Francisco during the war began to fill in some of this information for me.

I began to hear of Christian leaders who had gone to Bob Jones University. Outstanding personalities came to the YFC meetings and mentioned that they had attended Bob Jones.

Bob Jones, Bob Jones, Bob Jones — I heard the name so often that I came to believe that it must certainly be one of the most outstanding of Christian schools.

So when I began to feel the Lord leading me to go to a Christian school, I inquired at B.J.U. in South Carolina first.

You see how stupid I was?

I guess you know what Bob Jones had to say.

"Under no circumstances will we accept a black as a student at Bob Jones University."

I was stunned and shocked.

It hadn't even dawned on me that there was a color line in evangelical circles.

I will say this for B.J.U. They were not hypocrites. You knew exactly where you stood.

After that bomb from South Carolina, San Francisco looked better and better all the time. The independent church I had grown up in leaned toward the Assembly of God denomination and their Bethany Bible College was right in the city. Furthermore, my grandmother knew the school president.

Ultimately, I was more or less able to rationalize racial prejudice at B.J.U. They were right in the South and, furthermore, they did not have the emphasis on the ministry of the Holy Spirit that we had in our full-gospel circles.

I comforted myself by saying that surely racial prejudice wouldn't exist among people who claimed to be baptized in the Holy Spirit.

It seems a bit ludicrous now, but grandma took me by the hand and off I went to enroll in Bible college. I was twenty years old and had already been in the army. I had graduated from San Francisco State College, but we'll come to that later.

We were ushered into the president's office and grandma told prexy why we had come. I noticed a stunned and surprised look cross his face. I couldn't for the world know why.

Later in the conversation he said, "You realize that when you enroll you'll be our first Negro, don't you?"

No, I didn't realize it. But this didn't impress me somehow. I didn't weigh the statement. I had no reaction.

So I'm the first Negro, I thought. *Hurrah. Good. Great.*

The first wall in my life had started to crumble and I wasn't even impressed.

The first semester was deceptively free from racial overtones. It wasn't until later that I realized what head-scratching I was causing the administration as the second semester rolled around. My buddies filled me in.

Bethany was moving to its new campus in Santa Cruz some seventy-eight miles south of San Francisco for the second semester.

Because of this, their one black student would have to live on campus instead of in his own home. The issue was whether or not they could have a Negro living in the dormitory.

Who would room with a Negro?

The school had already — though perhaps reluctantly — enrolled me as a student and they didn't have any excuse for asking me not to return. My grades were good enough and my conduct record wasn't all that bad.

They finally decided that they had no alternative but to let me return.

But up to this day I can't help but laugh at the neat little solution they came up with to solve the roommate dilemma.

A Filipino brother was enrolling as a freshman that year — and they decided that since his skin was brown he probably wouldn't mind living with a Negro.

Of course I didn't mind rooming with a Filipino. This even had a providential twist as eventually I was to become a short term missionary to the Philippines.

But when I learned *why* I had been put with him I couldn't help but get the inference that since he was *only* a Filipino and I was *only* a Negro it would be okay for the two of us to live together.

My buddies never told me this, and perhaps it was never even discussed among the administration and faculty. But there is hardly a doubt in my mind but that the real problem was a boy-girl one. Since the campus was no longer in the city and not even in the small town of Santa Cruz proper, there would be great danger that I would be mixing socially with white girls.

What if Bob Harrison dated a white girl? And the unspeakable, unthinkable — what if he married one?

I strongly believe that everything else was really incidental to this main issue, whether spoken or not.

The problem never materialized, of course.

Later I would be victimized by other racial issues in the denomination but for the next two and a half years I passed my time deceptively free of racial overtones at the school.

20

CHAPTER FOUR

When Black Was Green

There were some rough spots, of course. My friends among the students and faculty, I learned now and again, protected me from many of the problems that could have hurt me.

They were sincere in this and I love them for it. But I sometimes think that it would have really been better to face these problems along the way. It might have been easier to accept the ultimate blow when it came.

In the school itself I got along handsomely. The students and faculty members came from all over the country and some had never known a Negro before. But they quickly saw that I didn't swing from trees with one hand while scratching my chest with the other.

I was very active in music and sports. Always an outgoing person, I love people and my life revolves around people. Because of these things I think it would not be improper or exaggerating to say that I became a popular student.

I was elected to the student advisory committee and was also elected vice-president of my class. Later I turned down the nomination for president of the student body.

My many activities just crowded me too much. Sometimes I had to miss a day or two of school because of traveling with various music groups. I was also busy arranging music for trios, for the choir, for our quartet and for other small groups.

I made special arrangements for instrumentalists to use as offertories. I represented the school as official pianist and official school baritone.

My athletic involvement was also time consuming.

So I turned down the nomination though I felt I might well have been elected.

I'm not trying to impress anyone with my popularity, only trying to show the kind of relationship I had on campus.

I developed some close friendships with faculty members as well.

Perhaps surprisingly, the two faculty members who meant the most to me were from Texas. After about two years in school, our friendships were so strong that they were able to give me some personal insights relating to the black-white issues.

"Bob," they said, "there will be people who cannot accept you as a person and as a Christian. They will see the exterior before they can feel the spirit of the interior."

They filled me in on the problems of the South that were now spilling over into the North and West. Their friendships were really enlightening. They gave me an exposure to areas of the black-white problem of which I had little or no understanding.

But I guess it is like everything else. You don't really learn until you begin to experience.

I didn't have to wait long for these experiences to start piling up, either.

Again I should say that my experiences of racial prejudice were nowhere near as extreme as those I would have had if I had grown up in the South.

But I believe that the problem of prejudice is actually more difficult in the North because it is so subtle and so white-washed. In the South one knows what to expect. It is no secret that there is a racial problem. A Negro would know that he is not welcomed in restaurants, hotels, even churches there. He knows about discrimination in schools and on jobs.

But the North says, "We don't have a problem."

The problem is there nonetheless.

For this reason, a racial incident can really be more traumatic for the Negro. In the South the Negro is prepared for abuse. But in the North and West he is not prepared. His defenses are down.

This would be all the more true in evangelical circles.

When I was really saved and ushered into a whole new life, I had a love and genuine concern for everyone. All the hatred for people below the Mason-Dixon line left. The prejudices, the snap judgments, the animosities were all gone.

Since this was my experience, I expected that all Christians would have this same transforming conversion.

When the Bible says that a man in Christ is a new creature and that the blood of Jesus cleanses us from all sin, I expected that this covered the racial sins as well.

But as I mature in my Christian life, I find that it is possible to hang on to our little pet sins and somehow justify them. These are the very sins, however, that quench and grieve the Spirit of God and thereby prevent His working as He wants.

The prejudice I found as I began venturing out from the school was subtle and many times clothed in hypocritical terms of praise and friendship.

But it isn't hard to see through this kind of sweet talk. The only ones being fooled are the ones working you over. They think they are being so clever, but they would be shocked at how much they are revealing of themselves.

Do they think we blacks are so stupid that we cannot see this?

A man in one church came up to me and said, "You cute little nigger, you. We certainly enjoyed that song you sang."

He was complimenting me, but he also was making sure I realized I was *only* a Negro.

"Even though you are here, remember you still have to stay in your place," he was saying in so many words.

As we traveled, I became more and more aware of a certain uneasiness that hovered around me. It dawned on me that I was not as welcome as I thought I would be.

This was especially noticeable when I traveled with the quartet. (I frequently went out alone as a singer and pianist, as well.) The pastor or leader would acknowledge and greet the quartet. Then he'd get around to me.

"And we are so glad to have our dear colored brother with us," they would say. "And we know there is no difference in us. We want our dear colored brother to know we feel there is no difference."

There was always this blabbing about "our dear colored brother." If they truly felt there was no difference why did they have to flagellate the point? They were simply making it quite clear that there are white Christians and there are black Christians.

This isn't just my personal hang-up. No black likes this form of paternalism. If you want to incite a dear colored brother, just call him a "dear colored brother."

I honestly feel that the apostle Paul wanted us to get

over the idea of feelings of racial superiority when he kept emphasizing the oneness in the body of Christ.

"There is neither Jew nor Greek, there is neither slave nor free, there is neither male nor female; for you are all one in Christ Jesus," Paul says (Gal. 3:28 RSV).

After a service in a church in Phoenix I was invited to a home for refreshments. Suddenly I realized that a number of the guests were off to themselves having some good laughs. They began telling a series of racial jokes, always about the darkie and a mammie. They kept on and on. It was very pointed. It was obvious that the whole thing was for my benefit.

Another time the quartet and I went to Southern California. When it came time to assign accommodations, we learned that the quartet was to stay in one home nearby and that I would stay clear across town. The meeting was in Hollywood and I was to stay in 122nd Street, about as far away as you can get in L.A.

And of course "it just so happened" that the people I stayed with were black. They tried to make it look as if this was just how it happened to work out.

You see how obvious it all is?

And the same Paul whom they love to quote to prove their own points says there is neither Jew nor Greek, bond nor free.

I felt sorry for the fellows in the quartet. They were always so embarrassed, and they'd always try to apologize.

But you can't do that.

"Look," I'd tell them. "No one can apologize for someone else's rudeness. I can't apologize for the blacks who are rioting and hating and acting without thinking. Neither can the white people of today apologize for the atrocities of the slave owners. You don't need to apologize for what others are doing to me."

But they always took it hard. Worse than I did.

By this point I thought I was at the place where racial incidents would not bother me. I thought I could just consider the source of each one, shrug my shoulders and go on serving the Lord without rancor.

That's how naive, how green I was.

I couldn't have been more wrong.

CHAPTER FIVE

A Little Black Boy Goin' Nowhere

It was Friday, just two weeks before graduation in June of 1951.

We seniors had finished all our classes, had turned in all our papers, and had taken all our exams.

I was set for my part in the graduation exercises which, as usual, was a musical one. I was going to sing in a small group and later sing a solo.

Earl Gould and Eddie Kramer and a couple of other guys and I were on our way to take care of one last appointment. All of us were planning on a full-time ministry with the Assemblies denomination and were on our way to meet the District committee. Our applications were already made and if we passed this interview we would be granted licenses to preach. This license would be good for about two years, after which we could become eligible for ordination.

Earl and Eddie and I were talking about our evangelistic plans. Our friendships had grown into a strong desire to serve the Lord together. We felt the Lord leading us to form an evangelistic team. Earl and Eddie

27

were good musicians who had been in our school quartet. I would provide added music as well as the preaching. We planned to work together for the summer and then see where it might lead.

All this hinged, of course, on being granted credentials. But there seemed to be no question in anyone's mind about this.

I hadn't gotten straight "A's" as Earl and Eddie had, but my grades weren't bad. And the affable, good-natured Bob Harrison hadn't gotten into trouble, either. On top of this, the school had used me to represent them all over the State.

As we got in line to wait our turn to go before the presbytery, I saw that my mother, along with my sister and godmother, was already waiting for me in the car. Since it was Friday, I would be going home for the weekend as soon as this one last chore was over.

My dear, godly mother. How proud she was to see me entering the ministry. I had sown my wild oats for years. How she had longed for and prayed for this day.

The line shortened quickly. Earl and Eddie went in ahead of me and came out smiling.

"I made it."

"Well, boy, we made it."

I went in next with a smile on my face, too. With great confidence I handed in my application along with the two dollar fee to the secretary-treasurer in the ante-room.

Then I marched into the den of lions.

I think there were four examiners in the room. They were all district officials. They represented northern California and Nevada. This was one of the strongest and largest districts in the denomination with nearly 400 churches.

"Well, Bob, we're proud of you, and we're glad for the grades you have and we've enjoyed your being in the school," the superintendent of the district intoned in his Arkansas drawl.

I squirmed a bit as he went on and on like this.

Why all the chit-chat, and the blah-blah and evasiveness with the line so long outside, I wondered.

They went on complimenting me and buttering me up.

With a certain gravity the superintendent picked up my application and said, "I see that you have made application for credentials."

Was he kidding? Were the kids coming in for anything else that day? Maybe he thought I was in the lunch line?

Then he looked me square in the eye and said, "I'm sorry, my brother (sic), but it is not the policy of our denomination to grant credentials to Negroes."

Just like that. That was it.

The bottom just fell out of my life.

I was shocked — literally speechless. I stood there like a statue.

He had to repeat his statement, because I didn't move, I didn't say a word.

I was so shocked there was nothing to say. I didn't question the statement, I didn't ask why.

After a few tense moments he quietly said, "You can step into the office and get your fee back. We're sorry."

After being stunned, I was now hurt and angry. I rushed out of the office. I didn't get the fee back. As I passed the secretary I might have said "keep it" or something like that. I don't know. I just rushed out.

I didn't say anything to the kids either. Some of them were asking, "Well, how did it go, Bob?" But I didn't say anything.

They began to realize that something was wrong. I wasn't the usual, happy-go-lucky Bob Harrison they knew.

After I had walked about a quarter of a block, uncontrollable tears began to roll down my face. I rushed straight for the car where my mother was waiting.

Without saying a word I got into the car and just started driving.

Naturally they knew that something was wrong. Mom guessed what had happened, but not the reason. My proud, gracious mother. She wouldn't press the issue. She just waited for me to compose myself so that I could tell what happened.

I drove for about half an hour, while the tears splashed down my face, before I could tell her the story.

At first I was really hurt. Crushed. I kept hearing the words, "I'm sorry, but it's not our policy to grant credentials to Negroes."

My hurt turned to bitterness.

I began to review all the injustices to my people over the centuries. Now to think that this had all slopped over into Christianity.

Especially full-gospel Christianity.

The more I thought about it, the more bitter I became. The bitterness welled up in me and finally I turned to my mother and said, "Well, I'm just not going back. I don't even care if I don't graduate."

But how does one say something like that to a mother like mine and get away with it?

"Son," she said, "you think about this and pray about it. Remember, if you don't go back and graduate then you may be further hurt and hindered in what God has for your life."

At home I headed straight for my room where I brooded for a couple of hours. Finally Mom came in and put her arm around me. We had a word of prayer and she tried to encourage me.

"Bob, you just have to realize that this is a part of

living. All is not joy and invariably there are storms. This is one of the severe testing grounds that God is allowing you to go through. What has happened is not right nor can it be justified.

"But you're not the first to have something like this happen and you'll not be the last.

"Now you must prove your strength in God and the reality of Christ in your life. If you overcome and become victorious in this, it will be a spiritual advantage for you."

But I wasn't ready for this. The bitterness engulfed me. It was eating me up. I had reached for the moon and almost touched it. Then all of a sudden I was nothing but a little black boy again.

A little black boy who was nothing and who could become nothing simply because he was black.

CHAPTER SIX

Growing Up Wasn't Easy

Of course, when I look back into the childhood and youth of that little black boy, I must admit it was really something that I came as close as I did to becoming a minister at this time.

Just growing up was tough enough.

Mom says I was only two when I came down with double pneumonia. We were living in a cold, dark apartment, and I probably wasn't getting the full nutrition I needed, either.

"Doctor, is he going to die?" Mom asked in quiet dignity.

"I'm sorry, mam, but I can't make any promises," the doctor answered. "Even if he does pull through it will be a miracle if he grows up to be a normal, healthy boy."

Now that was one thing I had going for me. It just so happened that my mother *did* believe in miracles.

Mom and dad prayed. I quickly mended after that, and have suffered none of the permanent effects the doctor had predicted.

I went back to live under the same conditions, of course. The place I remember best from those childhood days was a musty little basement apartment my sister and I and my mother and dad shared with the rats and roaches. We all suffered from severe colds, and tuberculosis was constantly nipping at our heels. I can remember living in seven such flats in my childhood.

As with many ghetto families, much of the burden of raising a family fell on my mother's shoulders.

Because of high rents and impossible purchase prices — not to mention the color of our skin — we were never able to move out of San Francisco's Fillmore area ghetto as such. But mother was determined that we would not live out our lives under the extreme conditions of those first years.

Life had not treated mom as cruelly as it had my father, so she had not lost hope, the one necessary ingredient in getting ahead. She was born in New Orleans to a Creole father and Negro mother. The family moved to the more healthful racial environment of the Pacific Northwest when she was still a baby, however, so she grew up with more optimism toward life.

It was harder for dad. His parents were also mixed racially — his father was one-half English but he grew up in the West Indies where the black was kept "in his place." He started out as a cook on ships going to South America and his blackness never let him out of the kitchen. He later cooked for a university in South America and then spent forty years as a chef with the Southern Pacific Railroad in California.

Because of his job, dad was gone much of the time and his paychecks were miserably small when he brought them home.

But mother threw herself into the task of improving our lot. She took in foster children and did sewing to keep the bills paid. She slashed our meager budget and stretched the money with the usual devices of the poor. We kept our shoes usable for many extra months by cutting out cardboard soles to place inside. During the rainy season we had to cut out a new sole from those carefully hoarded Shredded Wheat boxes every day.

Finally mother was able to move us into a more comfortable four-bedroom home and the days of hopping from one slum apartment to another were over.

The schools and the streets were just the same, though. In those days in San Francisco there weren't so many Negroes. We didn't have to go to an all-black school. We went to school with white kids. We even made friends and played with them. But when the last school bell rang for the day there was no hiding the fact that the white kids ran home to their nice neighborhoods and we trudged back to the filth. School was great make-believe. Even in those boyhood days we knew that dreams could come true if you had white skin but not if you were black.

So we blotted it all out by going back to our streets and getting into a fight. Someone was always challenging someone else. We fought every day. It was almost a sport like playing baseball or marbles.

I took my share of lumps, of course, but in the process I learned every type of street fighting and became one of the best fighters in the whole area. One thing led to another and pretty soon I found myself in a series of gang wars. I was fortunate in that the worst I ever suffered was a gash just below my eye which required eight stitches to close.

It could have been worse — had I been struck a quarter of an inch higher I would have lost the eye. But it was enough to make me get smart and look for some other way to become a big shot.

About this time I entered a junior high school where

they had an organized athletic program. This proved to be a better outlet for my abundant energy and my overpowering frustrations.

I tried out for basketball and baseball but I soon found that my greatest abilities were in track. I've been running almost as long as I've been walking, I guess. I ran wherever I went. One time mother sent me to the store for a couple bottles of milk. I ran to the store, of course, but I also ran home. In the process I stumbled and landed in the mass of glass from the breaking milk bottles. It took sixteen stitches to stem the flow of blood from the gash in my arm.

Other than that, running was a pretty non-violent sport and was good for me. I trained hard, even as a junior high kid. I developed into a pretty good sprinter and eventually won all-city and all-state medals.

In high school I continued as a successful runner and I also developed into the top halfback on the football team. I liked the excitement; I liked the attention. I swaggered around campus with my athletic letters prominently displayed.

Sports were a big factor in my life, but to understand why the ghetto didn't have an even stronger hold on me we'll have to talk about music. It's hard to be the neighborhood tough and the best pianist on the block at the same time.

How my mom scraped enough money together to buy a piano I'll never know. She's gone now, having died of cancer in 1962. (Dad died three weeks later — also from cancer.) But I bless her ten times a day for the sacrifices she must have made to bring a little music into the home.

It was an old upright with chipped ivories and never quite in tune. But when I sat up to it I could pick out the melodies that were running through my head.

Mom never wasted anything, and she wasn't going to waste any musical talent I might have. When I was nine she badgered a friend into giving me lessons. I've kept at it ever since. When I was in high school I was even able to study at the San Francisco Conservatory of Music.

Music didn't turn me into a saint, of course. In fact, for many years I believe it kept me from the Lord. I basked in one dream — that of becoming a great jazz musician. But in my church jazz and Christianity didn't mix. I had to choose between jazz and Christ. I chose jazz. Some blacks had made it in music and this became one crack in the door to let in a little light.

In more ways than one, music eventually would turn my life around, but in those high school days it just wasn't enough to blot out the curse of being black. Being black and being poor and living in segregation and discrimination was getting to me more and more. I would visit the homes of some of my white friends and see what they had. Then I would go home and be overwhelmed with the hopelessness of our situation.

There was my poor mother struggling against the inevitable. And where was dad? Not once did he ever see me in a track meet or watch me score a touchdown. He wasn't there to encourage me and he wouldn't have had he been there. His blackness trapped him in a menial job and he couldn't see how education was going to help me, either.

The whole load was becoming too much for me, so after my junior year in high school I dropped out and joined the army.

Maybe it wasn't the smartest thing to do, and I know that many people have been in tougher situations and made it through. But at least it gives me an understanding of today's school dropouts.

I've been there.

I've seen my mother go without needed clothes and other necessities just to keep my sister and me in school.

"All right," I said to myself. "What do I have to look forward to even if I do get an education? Mom and dad weren't able to make it. Look what little they have to show for years of perseverance and suffering.

"So I go to school. Will I be guaranteed a job like everyone else when I get out? Will I earn a good income? Can I buy a home any place I want? Will I have a good future for my children?"

I can well understand what goes through the minds of ghetto kids when there is so little to hope for.

There is no future, so they just drop out.

Who can blame them?

I was a dropout and I understand.

In my case I can't say that this was all bad, though. I joined the army and this was quite likely the salvation of me as a person.

The father authority figure that I so often found wanting in my own home I found, in overwhelming abundance, in the army. The army taught me to be a man.

In those days the service was still segregated so my officers and buddies were all Negroes. I could never say they were soft on me, but these guys understood what I was going through and wanted to help. The idea of being a soul brother is not just a convenient slogan. The suffering we have all shared draws us together on a gut level.

My officers and friends helped me develop a true sense of values and priorities.

"Man, if you're going to have any chance at all, you're going to have to get education," they said.

They were so convincing that I began taking high school correspondence courses and actually earned my diploma during the one year I was in the service. Now I couldn't wait to get out and start college.

But that's getting a little ahead of my story, for the army also revived my dreams of a musical career.

My first job after boot camp was in the transportation corps in a stevedore outfit. In other words, I was doing hard, manual labor. One of the early jobs was to help unload mustard gas bombs from a captured German ship.

Many of the bombs were leakers, so we wore gas masks and chemically treated clothing—something like the astronauts wear today. Even with all these precautions, many of us received burns. In my case, the gas permanently damaged the whites of my eyes and changed the color of my hair.

In the meantime I found out that there was a section of the army called Special Service. All I would have to do here, I learned, was to play the piano and percussion instruments.

Now this sounded a great deal more interesting than being slowly gassed to death by German mustard bombs.

The only hitch was that I had never in my life had a single lesson on percussion instruments. So, would you believe, I got a friend of mine quickly to teach me some of the basics of reading drum music? Then I went and took a test and bluffed my way into becoming a snare drummer in the percussion section of the base band.

Once I got into Special Service, you can bet your sweet life I didn't want to get kicked off this gravy train. I had bluffed my way in, but I knew I was going to have to study hard to stay in. Soon I would be playing not only in the marching band, but in the seventy-eight-piece concert orchestra. This would require abilities in snare drum, bass drum, cymbals, xylophone, timpani, and so on.

So I really worked. I spent hours at a time, every day.

You never know whom you are going to bump into in the army. I was in for some pleasant surprises. In this same outfit I found I was rubbing shoulders with some of the finest musicians from some of the outstanding bands in the country.

These included Count Basie, Duke Ellington and Lionel Hampton.

Well, I really learned a lot from these guys. Here was the little black boy who couldn't make it in the integrated school rubbing shoulders with some real musical big shots. The fact that they, too, were black convinced me I was going in the right direction.

I was really in a select section of the army. We had special privileges, and in our own way we were heroes.

It gave me a good feeling.

It gave me a sense of identity and respect.

A comforting ray of sunlight was beginning to dawn on my black night of despair.

I was on my way out of the tunnel.

My ambitions began to soar. I managed an early discharge and it was with a sense of elation that I enrolled in San Francisco State College as a music major. I was going to make a name for myself. I was going to make a pile of that green stuff, too. There would be no more ghetto life for me. I would pay back my mother for all the sacrifices.

The world was going to be my oyster after all.

Of course, I was reckoning all this without God. Before my dream would come true, He was going to get in His licks, too.

When God Was Sneaky

The army had been good for me and good *to* me. I could believe that Uncle Sam was black.

Music treated me well, too. Whatever I invested in it repaid handsome dividends. Maybe music was black.

My army buddies had convinced me that education was also on my side. I finished high school while in the army and rushed into college after my discharge. My music major required long hours of practice, and football and track at San Francisco State took up a lot of time, too. But I was so eager to reap the rewards of education that I took an accelerated course and graduated in three years at the age of twenty.

I was sure that education was going to do a lot for me. And anything that was going to help a Negro must be black.

But was God black?

It seemed that He had done a lot for the white folks. They were rich. They could become anything they wanted.

But what had He done for this little black boy?
What had He done for mom?

.We walked those fourteen blocks to church every Sunday and still managed to be the first ones there. We were the last ones to leave late that night, too.

For years my sister Florence and I had perfect attendance in Sunday school. Later on I was a leader in the youth group and I sang in the choir. We never missed a special service.

Each meal at home was like Sunday school all over again. We read the Bible, we talked about the Bible, and we memorized the Bible. By the time I was five I knew the books of the Bible and could recite Psalm 23, Psalm 1, Psalm 91, 1 Corinthians 13 and others.

But what had all this gained us? We didn't have a car, we didn't have fine clothes, dad couldn't get a better job.

Maybe Uncle Sam was black, and music and education were black. But not God. If He were black, would not He be doing something for us, too?

So education and music became the twin masters I served after getting out of the army.

I wanted to become a complete musician, so in school I studied woodwinds. I studied piano. I studied classical music and I studied every kind of jazz.

After school I pored over every book on any kind of music I could find. *Downbeat* magazine, the top periodical for jazz musicians, became my bible. I went to hear every musician who came to town, and then I would go home and try to imitate his style.

There were several of us in the neighborhood with this passion for music. We naturally gravitated toward one another.

Soon we were playing for dances and night clubs. I had it made because I could play both the piano and the drums. When someone didn't need a pianist to

When God Was Sneaky

complete his combo, he probably needed a drummer. When neither were needed I sometimes tried singing, though I never really took this seriously. I don't know why, because many thought I had a good voice and predicted that I could develop into an outstanding entertainer as a singer.

Johnny Mathis, who really made a big name for himself, was one of the guys in the neighborhood with whom I spent a lot of time. When we appeared together everyone said there were two boys who were really going places.

I began to make some of the money I had my eye on, but this wasn't the big thing. At least not yet. I worked hard and I studied hard because I knew all too well I was going to have to be better than the white boys studying music to get my foot in the door ahead of them.

Graduation day approached and an exhilarating sense of anticipation gripped me. I would soon be out of school and could just feel it in my bones that the good offers would be coming in.

I wasn't disappointed. One of the first offers was for $700.00 a week as a starter. That's $3,000.00 a month, more than my dad made all year. That's $36,000.00 a year. And it was only the beginning. The things I hadn't even dared dream about would all be mine.

But before I could get my jazz career off the ground, Someone interfered.

It was all kind of sneaky.

"So Bob likes music," the Lord must have said to my mother. "There's this Spanish musician who made quite a name for himself in the entertainment world. Now he belongs to me. You get your son down to the church when my musician is there and we'll see how strong a hold jazz has on him."

God's conversation with my mother must have gone

something like that, and mom was only too eager to listen.

I was still living under my mother's roof and I was still very close to her in spite of the fact I had not yet trusted the Lord. Not for one moment had I tried to give anyone the impression that I was a Christian. I guess there was this much fear of God in me. I didn't want to be a hypocrite. I had seen too many of these. Their Christian profession was as hollow as a bass drum.

But for mom's sake, I didn't hesitate when she asked me to attend an evangelistic rally on a Sunday afternoon a few weeks before graduation. My plan was to attend the rally, sit in the back and then leave when everyone was absorbed in the meeting. There was a four-hour jam session planned for that afternoon and I didn't want to miss it.

No one hurt, everyone happy.

The rest of the afternoon I just can't explain. My mind was on the jam session. But suddenly I found my attention riveted to the service. The hymns I had heard and sung hundreds of times without noticing before became very personal. They all seemed to be aimed directly at me. They pointed to the love of God, to the patience of God, to the forgiveness of God. In return for all these, I realized, I hadn't been willing to give God the time of day. I had not even said "thank You" for a breath, much less anything else.

A final blow was struck by George Morales, the Spanish soloist who had been converted from the entertainment world. Using his guitar as accompaniment, he got up and sang, "I trust in God, I know He cares for me."

During that first verse it seemed that my whole life up to that moment flashed before me. It added up to a big fat zero.

I had drawn everything on the bank of heaven, but had deposited nothing.

God had given me a godly home. He had given me loving parents who sacrificed for me. He had given me a fine Christian background and a good education.

It struck me also that He had given me my musical talent. He gave it to me but I was planning to use it only for myself.

George sang the second verse. I began to realize that God did care for Bob Harrison. Bob Harrison personally. Not just the Harrison family.

I realized that I had found God's Son in the church building, I found His Son in the hymns being sung, I found His Son even in the solos.

But His Son could not be found in my heart.

About the third verse of that song the Holy Spirit came with great convicting power. I realized that all I knew about Christ didn't add up to a personal possession of Christ.

Before that Spanish singer finished the last verse, I knew I had to accept Christ personally.

Without a counselor, without a message, I accepted Jesus as my Lord and Savior.

I stayed for the rest of the service without being aware of what was being said or done. I do know that uncontrollable tears rolled down my cheeks. First they were tears of repentance and then tears of joy.

I was ushered into a place of spiritual ecstasy.

What did education matter? What was so great about becoming a famous jazz musician? What good was a lot of money?

I had seen God and these things were tinsel by comparison.

God loved me and now He dwelt within me.

God was black!

My mother must have sensed what had happened.

I saw her get up in front of me and I thought she was heading for the rest room. But she came directly to me. She saw the tears in my eyes and recognized immediately that the great transformation had taken place.

She put her arms around me and prayed. She encouraged me to make a public acceptance of the Lord. This I did at the end of the service.

Needless to say, I didn't make it to the jam session that day. When the guys asked why, I told them that I had accepted Christ as my Savior and had become a Christian.

That got a laugh and the old hee-ho. But it didn't change my stand.

Just two months after my conversion the agent rang my doorbell and made the seven hundred buck offer. It was tempting. Very tempting. I didn't say no right away. I fumbled around and talked around.

But during the course of the conversation I finally said, "No, I couldn't. My church wouldn't permit it."

It was a pretty chicken testimony, but I think the Lord had pity on me, knowing that this was my first test and that I was just a babe in Christ. Later on, I did sense a spiritual reward for just saying no.

More offers came in from time to time. I told the agents that I had accepted Christ into my life and didn't feel that I could take Him into theaters and night clubs.

The more I said no, of course, the stronger I became.

Sessions with my musician friends dwindled. I had not dropped them right away but the old jazz world was losing its pull on my life.

By the time five or six months had gone by, I had a strong conviction that God wanted me in full-time ministry.

So I turned my back on popularity, I turned my back on what had been the greatest desire in my life. The world had strongly beckoned with its allure of fame and fortune. Now I turned my sights toward the Christian school I knew would prepare me to be an effective servant for Jesus Christ.

This is where I really belonged.

I was home at last.

Now, life would be beautiful.

CHAPTER EIGHT

Up Off the Floor

For three years it *was* beautiful.

I basked in the fellowship and activities of Bible school. I dreamed beautiful dreams of zealously serving the Lord with the talents He had given me. The sacrifices were made but they were made with light-hearted abandon.

But the three years passed and with their passing came that fateful Friday before graduation when the sky fell in. Suddenly I was ready to wipe the whole experience right off the record. I was ready to forget Christianity and all it stood for.

I had a year in the army, a degree from San Francisco State, an exhilarating experience with the Lord, and a Bible school diploma behind me. But nothing ahead of me.

I was in the desert of despair — disgusted with Christianity, disgusted with my black self. I was disgusted with everything.

I was moping around the house one day when the

mailman came. There was a letter for me from Elmer Bueno, a Bible school buddy.

More condolences, I thought. *Who needs them?*

Without any enthusiasm I sliced open the envelope and found I was invited to be the guest speaker at the Calvary Church in East Oakland.

That was funny. Really funny. I gave a derisive snort.

"What is it?" Mom wanted to know.

"This black reject is invited to preach at an evangelistic service," I snarled.

Mother put her arm around me. "You can't be like that, son," she said. "What God has appointed no man can nullify. The call of God is still on your life. Give Him a chance to prove it."

Where would I be without this godly, patient, loving mother? Not an ounce of bitterness in her frail body.

In those first weeks mom encouraged me and prayed for me and took me to church. Little by little spiritual sensitivity and concern began to return.

I accepted the invitation and a couple of weeks later found myself in the pulpit again. I felt like an intruder. But as I spoke, some of the old fervor came back. I could sense that God was moving in the audience. At the invitation, several came forward.

With this encouragement, I began accepting other invitations, including one for a week-long revival series. A pianist friend of mine, Emanuel Williams, was on his summer vacation from the University of California, so I asked him to accompany me.

In spite of my denomination, and — more significantly — in spite of myself, I had suddenly become a member of a two-man evangelistic team. Just six weeks had passed since my dream had died in the conference room at Bethany Bible School.

The week was a success and Emanuel and I began accepting invitations which took us up and down the coast of California and Oregon. I was still occasionally engulfed by bitterness, but much to my surprise and chagrin, God really blessed. Sinners were being converted and church members revived.

I had been through a spiritual street fight and had been roughed up pretty badly. I had been knocked down but not out. I had fought the toughest guy on the block and survived. The rest of the way out would be easier now.

Besides putting me back on my spiritual feet, that first summer spent as a traveling evangelist brought a couple of other things that would have life-time consequences.

One resulted from the fact that Emanuel was such an excellent pianist. Because of this, I began to devote all of my musical attention to singing. For the rest of my life it would be my singing as much as anything that would open doors for me — organizational doors as well as doors to people's hearts.

The second resulted from the fact that we began to receive as many invitations to black churches as white. Among other things Pastor Miller had in his black church in Pasadena, California, was a beautiful daughter — and a member who liked to play cupid.

The latter asked me if I would mind taking Marilyn Miller out to dinner. I thought over the proposition — for about a tenth of a second — and then answered in a manner that I hoped appeared casual and unconcerned, "No, not at all."

As subsequent meetings took me to Southern California I managed to meet Marilyn again and again. Eight months later we became engaged and a year after that, on July 6, 1952, we were married.

I wasn't offering my new bride much of a life, or much of a future. By this time I had accepted the invitation to become associate pastor of a little ghetto church in San Francisco. "Emmanuel Church" the sign bravely announced in front, but it still looked more like the two-story Victorian house it had formerly been.

The pastor was old, and the few people still attending were pretty set in their humdrum ways. Each time I would try something different or new, someone would say, "Oh, you're just trying to be smart since you just graduated from school."

It hardly seemed a church which could support an assistant let alone a full-time pastor. It didn't take me long to find that they couldn't. My "salary" was $55.00 a month. I took a job in the post office, but they didn't pay too much in those days either. I was bringing Marilyn into a pretty tight economic situation.

We rented a little two-room apartment for $57.00 a month. There was a kitchenette and a living room that converted into a bedroom at night. The divan became a bed. Even $57.00 was too much on our salary, so we began to look for something else.

In the process of looking, I was brought up-to-date on the racial situation in San Francisco. By now the black population in the city had swelled by many thousands. High wages paid by San Francisco shipyards during World War II had brought in a flood of southerners, both black and white.

The wartime solution for housing this great influx was to put up emergency and temporary apartment buildings. Blacks, naturally, were channeled into certain such apartment projects and whites into others. How easily and quickly were new ghettos born.

The project where we finally found an apartment to match our pocketbooks was an eyesore. The "temporary" housing of 1942 had become the permanent black slum of 1954. Thrown together in a hurry with inferior materials, these disintegrating buildings were now held together by little more than fading, peeling yellow paint.

It was another two-room apartment we were moving into, but it was a little larger and a little cheaper.

It was hardly the place to bring up the three children who were born to us here. Among our immediate neighbors were winos, prostitutes and other ne'er-do-wells grovelling through life on various forms of government aid.

The fellow next door was an alcoholic whose little toy was a .38 revolver. This didn't give me much comfort when I had to be gone.

Above us lived a family with three teenagers who played their deafening music for what seemed an endless round of parties and dances. There were times when we wished they were that wide-awake in the daytime! Among their lapses was the time they left the apartment with the water (they had been washing clothes) still running. It overflowed the sink and began filling up the room. Since we were immediately below them, the ceiling sagged and the water dripped through. We thought the whole thing was going to drop on us.

Such was life in the ghetto. Living with poor people is no problem in itself. But these poor blacks had their economic problems compounded by their social and racial problems.

Our physical surroundings were matched only by that which went inside us. A mental picture that endures is that of Marilyn putting our meat on the stove before noon so that it might be tender enough by night. Not that this always helped. No amount of cooking could turn some of that leather into food.

We survived, of course, and the children grew up normal and healthy. But sometimes the contrasts were very pointed. I had kept in touch with many of my school chums and we were invited to their homes on occasion. Most of them had become associate pastors of good churches and lived, if not elegantly, at least quite comfortably.

We were so ashamed of our living conditions that we wouldn't even bring friends near the apartment. Once friends were in our car with us when I had to stop home for something. I parked about two blocks away and ran back for it. It was that bad.

The old bitterness was not too far from the surface on occasions like this. *Wouldn't I be living in the same plush situation as these guys if my skin had not just happened to be dark?* I would ask myself.

Looking back on this period of my life, I get a completely different perspective. Living in the ghetto, scrimping on food, tripping over winos, all these played a tremendous role in preparing me for a future ministry of which I wasn't even thinking at this time.

The lack of official denominational recognition didn't hurt that much either. Mom was right. It wasn't a piece of paper on which man wrote that made the difference. It was the call of God on my life. The Lord didn't mind that I was only a black — because He was black, too.

Another thing they couldn't take away from me. Bethany really was a good Bible school. They had taught me well. I was prepared to step into this little ghetto church and build it up.

When the old pastor retired and I took over in March of 1955, I threw all my energies and talents and training into reviving the church.

To start with there was an average of about twenty-two in Sunday school and maybe twice that many in the morning worship. The church had been converted from an old house and could hold about two hundred in the "sanctuary." There were three other small rooms that were used for Sunday school.

The church wasn't much physically, but it was in a

strategic location on a corner close to good public transportation. There were schools and a huge housing project near by.

We were the only evangelical church trying to meet the needs of this ghetto and the growth of the congregation would have to come from the dregs of this black community.

James Williams (not his real name) was one of our first converts and he set the pattern for the kind of ministry we would have.

Someone had pointed him to our apartment. When I answered his knock I opened the door to a homeless, penniless, destitute dope addict.

Dope, I learned, had led him to the end of a dark alley and he was groping for some way out. He confessed to me that he had become an enemy of society and of himself. Was there any hope for him?

There certainly was. I introduced him to my Jesus that day. He didn't commit his life to Him at the time, but he kept coming back to hear more. After a few weeks he finally came to the church and at the invitation came forward.

His life was transformed, but not immediately.

It is relatively easy to preach the Gospel from a very secure spot behind the pulpit, but it's much harder to become really involved in lives. To have a ministry in the ghetto — or anywhere for that matter — one must be involved.

When James had first come to our apartment, we fed him and found him a place to stay. Now, as a babe in Christ, he needed more help than ever. The real battle was just beginning as he immediately realized that he would have to go through the painful withdrawal from dope.

I spent night after night with him, sometimes as late as three or four in the morning. I was with him when the monkeys were on his back. I saw the anguish in his eyes and on his face as his body was wracked with torture.

The grace of Jesus Christ brought him through. He kicked the habit. I was able to get a good job for him and eventually he married one of the outstanding teachers of the city of San Francisco. They have a beautiful child.

Most of all, he deeply loves the Lord. A young black who had been no more than a smelly wound in the flesh of society had found himself and become a productive and happy family man through the transforming power of Jesus Christ.

This kind of thing happened over and over again as the Sunday school grew to an average of around two hundred and the worship service and membership grew proportionately.

There were women living with common-law husbands who found Christ. There were many drunkards, gamblers and winos whose lives were changed by the Savior.

We were getting converts before they reached this point also. Street urchins and despondent students ready to drop out found Christ and swelled the rolls of the church.

As I look back on the five years spent pastoring this church from 1955-1960, I must admit to myself that these were exciting years. They weren't glamorous and it's not easy ministering to the needs of destitute people who have been forgotten by the rest of society. But I was growing and learning and constantly having the thrill of seeing God work His miracles.

One of the lessons I learned while ministering in the ghetto was that Jesus Christ Himself really is the answer to our social and economic problems.

Of course I'm not against the law makers and the

agencies who are trying to provide better schools, better jobs, better housing and a better life for our minority groups. But my ghetto experiences have led me to the firm conviction that we can only solve the basic problems of our society by changing people from the inside.

How much social gospel, how many tens of thousands of dollars, how much energy would it have taken to get a man such as James Williams off dope? All of man's resources could have been lavished on him without transforming his life as Jesus did at the church altar.

Many of the people who were coming into our church were the very ones causing our social ills. When Jesus touched their tattered lives a miracle took place. Their habits changed, their behavior patterns changed, their family outlook changed. They received a new image of themselves. From being leeches sucking out the life-blood of our society they became productive members of it.

Our experience was in just one little church on one corner of one small ghetto. But the experience provides the kernel truth of the only way out of the vast economic, social and racial problems that are lashing our nation.

What America needs is to see the church of America revived and involved in a great evangelistic awakening. To help the black man we are going to have to see tens of thousands of blacks come to know Jesus as their personal Savior.

That's why my purpose in writing is not to promote integration in our churches but to awaken black and white Christians to the real need of the hour.

In saying this, I am not denying the need to clean up our ghettos which breed the gangs and fights I have been describing. But cleaning up conditions will be meaningless if lives are not cleaned up as well — and

Jesus Christ is the only answer here. Evangelicals must become involved in both aspects of the clean-up.

Our real need is to mobilize and equip and train every black Christian and every white Christian in America to bring multitudes to the feet of the Savior.

I know my people can do their part because I saw it happen. When they came to know the Lord their interest was no longer focused on themselves but on others. Even in their poverty I saw converts and church members dig deeply into their pockets to help pay gas and electric bills for those even worse off. They raised money for food for those who were in need. They raised money for new chairs as the size of the congregation grew. They raised money for carpeting and for paint and eventually for another building as our Christian education program expanded.

Those who literally didn't have any money to give still wanted to participate. They gave of their time and energy. Several times we had cake and pie sales to raise funds. People who had been transformed by the power of Jesus were eager to be involved in reaching others in any way they could.

This encourages me. I know that if we really put our minds to it we can not only evangelize our people, but we can send out missionaries to the corners of the world.

I was learning these lessons in Fillmore and in the process I was coming more and more out of my own bitterness. I accepted and then learned to love the little church into which my black skin had forced me. I was eager to serve the Lord in Emmanuel Church for the rest of my life, if that was what the Lord wanted.

But without my knowing it, these five struggling, eventful and ultimately successful years as a pastor were drawing to a close.

God had other plans for this little black boy from the ghetto.

CHAPTER NINE

Pre-Fab Walls

Some of the walls holding back evangelical blacks have been pre-fabricated.

They are walls made up ahead of time and kept on the ready to block the path of any Negro getting too spiritually "uppity."

One of these is the notion that blacks can have an effective ministry only with other blacks. If an enterprising black Christian feels called to foreign missionary work, or wants to minister in white churches or join any number of evangelical organizations, this pre-fab wall is hastily set in the way.

"Don't you think you would have a more effective ministry among your own people?" he is asked.

Like many clichés, this rhetorical question has a kernel of truth.

And a bushel of error.

It's inconsistent. White missionaries, for instance, can have an effective ministry with red or yellow, black or white. But blacks, for some strange reason, can minister only to other blacks.

I had found out I couldn't be a black preacher in a white denomination. That round had been lost and I wasn't trying to get into the ring again. The ministry at Emmanuel was fully satisfying and the Lord had taught me some big lessons about pride.

But the desire to be an evangelist had never left me. The pastorate had taught me so much about people which I couldn't hope to learn in an itinerant ministry, but deep down inside I felt this wasn't the place I really ought to be. When I accepted occasional invitations to speak at evangelistic rallies and crusades it was like coming home.

Then came the day in 1958 when I was invited to sing and give my testimony at a huge Fourth of July camp meeting held by the Assemblies of God in Santa Cruz.

Among the four or five thousand who attended was Dr. Ben Kumerfelt, a former professor of mine at Bethany. He had returned to his native Germany and now was visiting just briefly in the States.

"Bob," he said after we had reminisced about our days at Bethany, "I was quite impressed with your testimony and singing. Have you ever given any thought about coming to Europe for a time of ministry?"

"The idea has never crossed my mind," I said.

"Well, you ought to pray about it," he said.

I just laughed it off. Negroes are forever being made big promises by guilt-ridden whites.

"Ah, sure. I'll think about it," I said. "It would be pretty nice."

At one time the idea would have seemed great. But the mental picture of this rejected black preacher standing before his ghetto congregation in an old house in Fillmore sounded pretty remote from Europe. After the conversation I forgot about it.

But about four months later I received a letter from

Dr. Kumerfelt and two other evangelical leaders in Germany. They were inviting me to come for a series of meetings.

I guess in Europe they hadn't received the word that I could have a ministry "only among my own people."

They were really backward. "Your singing and speaking coupled with the fact that you would be the first Negro ever to have a public ministry here would draw great crowds and result in many conversions," they said.

"We've seen Negroes in the field of entertainment and athletics," they wrote, "but we've never seen a black in Christian ministry."

This kind of argument really got to me. How many times since Bethany days had I thought about the church so often being behind the rest of the world in important social matters? The world was sending Negroes overseas, but the church was keeping its black Cinderellas in the attic.

It had been twenty-two years since Jesse Owens had demolished Hitler's absurd boastings that Negroes were sub-human in those 1936 Olympic games. But not a single black had been there in the meantime to preach Jesus Christ.

The white propaganda that I would not be effective overseas had already brain-washed me, and, as we'll see later, most other black evangelicals. I really had never thought of making such a trip.

I was about to learn that these pre-fabricated walls can be blasted apart just as easily as they can be thrown together — if a black is gutsy enough to test them.

Since this had come as an official invitation, Marilyn and I had to take it seriously. We prayed over and over that God would show us His will. He brought nothing to mind that in any way cautioned against my going, so I made arrangements for my church and accepted the invitation to be in Europe for the months of September, October and November of 1959.

All the personal assurances and logic and prayer, however, couldn't completely remove the anxiety from my heart as I got on the 707 bound for Germany. One might be convinced of God's protection in every circumstance, but that first step into a lion's den can be rather disconcerting.

Could a thousand voices telling the Negro that he and his ministry would not be welcomed overseas be wrong?

Would there be no trace of Hitler's racism left in the German heart and mind?

It was a nervous Negro at his window seat as the plane came in for a landing in West Berlin.

It was wasted worry.

I stepped off the plane and was greeted by a crowd welcoming me not with polite handshakes but with enthusiastic bear hugs.

I was a son safely home from the war.

I was a beloved brother returned from a distant land.

I was astounded and shocked. Everyone wanted to touch me. Some of it was curiosity, of course, but I sensed sincerity and affection.

I knew immediately that the thousand voices had all been wrong.

I jumped into this my first foreign adventure with a gleeful relish. This undoubtedly helped my rapport with the people.

When I first arrived I was given the choice of staying at a hotel or with a German family. I immediately chose the German family, even though they could speak no English and I could speak no German.

They greeted me at the front door with a well practiced "Goot bye, Broder." We had a good laugh together when they realized their mistake. This was going to be an adventure for them, too.

I bounced around this friendly little home with my Berlitz book on conversational German. By laboriously searching through it, I was able to come to agreement with my new German friends that I would try and teach them some English if they would teach me some German.

We got along famously. I never wanted for anything, as I was always able to get my thoughts across through the use of the little book. I learned some German and they learned some English.

This was a big help to me in the nightly crusade meetings as well. Every night I would try to use a new German phrase. They greeted my stumbling efforts with laughter and love and I think this broke down a lot of barriers. They could see I was really trying if nothing else. I even sang some Negro spirituals for them in German. They seemed to understand and were apparently moved by the emotional tone of them as well.

I spoke every night for two weeks at this crusade which was being held in the popular Nollendorff district of West Berlin. A speaker can usually sense the attitude of his audience even if his message is being interpreted — in this case by a woman — for him.

They were warm, friendly and hungry audiences. I was impressed by the number who came up after the service just to shake my hand and have prayer together. I could sense that God had used my ministry to touch their hearts. They felt my love and concern and wanted to feel this in a more personal way by having prayer together.

Hearts of sinners were touched too. I don't know exactly how many came forward that week, but there must have been at least five or six hundred who made first time decisions for Christ.

These German Christians had done their work well and the meetings were well covered by the local press. They made much of the fact that I was the first Negro minister to preach in Germany and they patted their country on the back for the great progress they had made since that eventful 1936 Olympics and Jesse Owens.

With the success of the crusade and the news stories I began to receive invitations from all over Germany and Switzerland as well as England. I ended up taking meetings in such Black Forest cities as Stuttgart, Karlsruhe, Lörrach and Freiburg. What exotic places they were. Did the ghetto of San Francisco really exist?

Word spread to the American military and I was soon ministering at Warner Concern, the American military base in Munich, and at a serviceman's retreat in Berchtesgaden, made famous by Adolf Hitler who had his Eagle's Nest hideaway there.

On the way home from Germany I had meetings in Zurich, Switzerland, and London, England.

Germany will always have a special place in my heart and I have since made five trips there. It was Germany that showered me with love and made me feel that I would never be a stranger in a foreign country. It was Germany, at least for me, that exploded the myth that a Negro can have an effective ministry only among his own people. And it was Germany where the revolutionary thought that it might be an *advantage* to be black first popped into my mind. My skin color was a passport to people's hearts even as my U.S. passport was effective in entering a country. This bold idea would ultimately redirect much of my energies for the rest of my life.

CHAPTER TEN

Africa the Beautiful

I was just beginning to come down out of the clouds and back to the realities of my pastoral duties at Emmanuel in San Francisco when another letter arrived that sent me through the same emotional changes as that first invitation from Germany.

This one was from Dr. V. Raymond Edman who was writing in his capacity as Chairman of the Board of the Billy Graham Evangelistic Association. The Association was asking me to join with Dr. Howard Jones in representing them in a ministry in Africa.

I had admired Dr. Edman's writings and his leadership as president of Wheaton College from a distance. And of course the name "Billy Graham" had represented the highest and best to this young black aspiring to be an evangelist. Now I had begun a personal correspondence with Dr. Edman, one of the spiritual giants of our generation, about a ministry under the sponsorship of Billy Graham, the greatest evangelist of our time.

Marilyn and I were astonished and overwhelmed. We were deliriously happy. We were scared to death.

We were so excited that we wanted to write back immediately and seal the agreement before they changed their minds.

But Dr. Edman had asked us to spend much time in careful prayer before we made any decision. Our first impulsive reaction was a human one and we knew it. Actually, Marilyn and I had grown spiritually to the place where we absolutely wanted to put God first in our lives regarding any decision.

We put Him first regarding our children; we put Him first in buying furniture. Nothing was too big or too small to lay at His feet. Our family verse had become Proverbs 3:5 and 6 which we still quote around our family table: "Trust in the Lord with all thine heart; and lean not unto thine own understanding. In all thy ways acknowledge Him, and He shall direct thy paths."

We prayed and corresponded with Dr. Edman for several weeks. Finally we disentangled all our various motivations and felt the Lord clearly saying that I should make the trip.

With our positive answer, the Graham organization then made detailed inquiry into my educational background and spiritual experience and ministry.

When they were convinced that this trip to Africa was truly the will of God, the preparations were made and I stepped forth on this venture into my ancestral past.

The trip was made with Dr. Howard Jones, who by this time had become the first black associate with the Billy Graham team.

Howard had bumped into a few walls of his own along the way. He was pastoring the Christian and Missionary Alliance Smoot Memorial Church in Cleveland, but for years the burden of ministering to black Africans had weighed heavily on him. The policy of this great Missionary denomination, however, stipulated that no Negroes could be sent to Africa.

The CMA was perhaps a bit ahead of the Assemblies in relationship to Negroes. They did grant him credentials and ordained him. Beyond this point, however, their logic was confusing. He could minister to blacks in America, but he could not minister to blacks in Africa, nor to whites anywhere. When God was black in the CMA He was consigned to the American ghetto.

But the burden persisted and when Howard read in a Christian magazine that station ELWA in Monrovia, Liberia, wanted tapes of an American Negro choir to play on the radio, Howard jumped at the chance.

He quickly put together a tape and sent it to Dick Reed, a Sudan Interior Missionary and ELWA station manager.

Reed played it, liked it, and asked for more.

Next they asked Howard to include some speaking on a tape. This received such a fine reception in Africa that the Sudan Interior Mission extended an invitation to Howard to speak in some meetings there.

He thus became the first American Negro to minister in Africa. It was a great eye-opener to him, to the S.I.M., and to the many others who saw how the hand of God was using this American Negro among the Africans.

A frequent rationalization used to keep American blacks out of Africa is that the Africans did not want us there. The argument went like this: If American Negroes went to Africa they would want to live on the same standard as any other white missionary. The African wouldn't want that. Since the American Negro was black, they would expect him to live like the black African. Therefore, it would be impossible, we were told, to have an effective ministry there.

Jones exposed this argument for what it was: an

empty theory. He was most eagerly welcomed wherever he went. His evangelistic crusades were fantastically successful and led to bigger things for him.

For while Howard was ministering in Africa, Billy Graham was preparing for his first New York City crusade. Billy had become concerned about integrating his evangelistic team, especially for this crusade which would encompass huge numbers of blacks and other minority groups.

He was casting about for the right black to join his team when Jack Wyrtzen brought up the name of Howard Jones. In the final decision, the fact that Howard had so eminently proved his success in having a ministry to blacks in Africa undoubtedly played a significant part.

Jones worked with Billy in an unofficial capacity in New York and then in the Cow Palace in San Francisco in 1958. It was after this later crusade that Howard officially became an associate evangelist with the team.

Another wall had been broken down.

As a San Francisco pastor at that time, I became involved in the Cow Palace crusade and worked especially in getting black churches involved. Naturally, I worked closely with Howard. We became fast friends as we ministered side by side and we did have some success. This undoubtedly played a large part in my being contacted by Dr. Edman in 1960 to go with Howard to Africa.

This was my second international trip, and the excitement of world travel had not yet become the routine which would characterize my life in the years following. But this was the trip to beat all trips. If our plane had crashed on leaving Africa, I would have died a happy and contented man.

As Howard had briefed me, the warm glow of the Africans engulfed us from the very moment we arrived at radio station ELWA in Monrovia, Liberia, our first stop. The national workers greeted us with glee and joy written all over their faces. I hadn't yet preached a word or sung a single song, so they didn't know if I were worth listening to or not. But they didn't seem to care. Just the fact that their black brothers had come from America was enough.

Our ministry began with a city-wide crusade in Monrovia and naturally we did a great deal of radio work with ELWA as well. Then we were asked to join Dr. Clyde Taylor, head of the National Association of Evangelicals, for some pastors' conferences in Nairobi, Kenya.

While there I was invited to speak and sing for some other meetings in Kenya, and these eventually developed into a full scale, city-wide crusade. The crusade, by the way, was sponsored by the Anglicans, Southern Baptists, Methodists, and the African Inland Mission — a pretty interesting bit of integration in itself.

From there, Howard and I went to Ethiopia and Uganda in East Africa, and then back to the west coast and Ghana and Nigeria and finally back to Liberia.

Sometimes Howard and I worked together and sometimes I was completely on my own. When we were together, I sang and played the piano and trained the choirs. When I was alone I still was greatly involved in the music and, of course, I also did the preaching.

As we traveled I was amazed to learn that many times we were the first American blacks our African audiences had ever seen. With tears in their eyes, the folks would ask us through their interpreters, "What has taken you so long to come? We heard that we had black sisters and brothers in America and we wondered why they never came over to tell us about Christ."

We learned, by the way, that the African had been told that American Negroes did not want to come to Africa, that he was ashamed of Africans.

We, of course, had been led to believe that we would not be welcomed in Africa. It was a neat little package with no loose ends.

The Africans asked us why we hadn't come sooner. I began to wonder myself why I hadn't.

We were so wanted. We were so needed. We were so loved.

Over and over the people would say to us, "Why haven't you come sooner? Can't you stay longer? Won't more of our black brothers and sisters in America come to share the Gospel?"

We'd be in one meeting and they would want us to go to another meeting in another tribal area. They would say, "There are many many more members of our tribe who have never heard the Gospel. Can't you please stay longer?"

Of course they identified readily with the color of our skin. But they seemed to be so genuinely excited about the fact that we were their American brothers.

I was very impressed by what missionaries had accomplished in Africa. What they have done in bringing the Gospel as well as education and agriculture and modern science is fantastic.

But the only missionaries Africans had ever seen were white. They loved and respected and responded to most of these, of course, but their indentification with the American black was so much more basic, I realized.

Maybe I should have expected this warmth from the Christian nationals. What was even more exciting was to see the enthusiastic reactions from all Africans as we began traveling and ministering out in the villages.

I'll never forget the official reception we received in a little village near Takoradi in Ghana. Our missionary companion drove us out into the jungle to a tribal group with whom he was acquainted. The rutted jungle road suddenly broke into a little clearing where we could see a number of thatched-roof huts.

The paramount chief came out to greet us in his multi-colored robe. It was a one-piece affair that had a slit for his head and hung all the way to the ground. His face was lined with tribal markings. The one incongruous accoutrement of his chief's position was the 1958 station wagon parked next to his grass hut.

He greeted us in a few words of broken English and then told us through the missionary interpreter how glad he was that we had come. He asked our permission to give us an official reception. We were elated with the idea.

His drummer pounded out a message telling the leaders of all the sub groups to assemble. I was fascinated with the drums themselves and asked if I could try them out. They were made of wood and skin and each of the two gave a different note.

Within fifteen minutes all his tribal council had arrived and squatted in a circle. They also bore the tribal markings on their faces and wore the brightly colored robes that had been woven and dyed with jungle materials. We were introduced individually to these council members who rose to shake our hands and give the broadest smiles I have ever seen.

Then the drummer began again and soon hundreds of tribal people came pouring out of the jungle from all directions. The American Negro has always been given credit for having tremendous rhythm, but when these tribal people began to dance I found out what rhythm was all about. I was absolutely amazed at the ability of the drummer and the dancers. Their sense of rhythm was fantastic. I realized that the American Negro had only a little bit left over from his ancestry in Africa.

We greeted the people and told them about our meetings in Takoradi, more than fifteen miles away. Many of them walked all the way to the meeting that night so they could hear their black brother from the United States tell the good news about life in Jesus Christ. A number of them became Christians.

Africa is colorful and beautiful. The continent contains the most beautiful scenery I have ever seen in my travels around the world. Even the streets of the cities are alive with color as the people mill about from shop to shop. Their flowing robes are bright and gay and boisterous.

What a sight it was when these Africans gathered by the thousands in some of our meetings. They rocked back and forth while singing the great hymns. The gentle hillsides became stadiums covered with the earth's gaudiest wild flowers bursting forth in song as they were caressed by a gentle breeze.

The American Negro has this same custom of swaying back and forth during congregational singing. I had assumed this came from slavery days, from a people mourning their fate and longing for that day of release.

But I see it is not. It comes from Africa, from a people expressing their faith and their joy in a living God.

After their singing, it was easy for me to get up and minister in song. They loved it when I sang the Negro spirituals. If they knew the song, they would spontaneously sing it with me. Many times they would know it in their own dialect, and there would be many dialects represented. In one meeting in a later trip to Sierra Leone there were 18,000 people singing a spiritual with me in 6 different dialects at the same time. They clapped in rhythm and did whatever I did. They took me right into their hearts. It was as if I were one of them, which I guess was partly true.

I'd kid about this between numbers. "You can look at me and tell that I'm not all African," I'd say. "I'm not all black. I'm kind of mixed-up. But I want you to know that somewhere way, way back my ancestry goes back to Africa."

They would laugh and clap at this. "Now remember," I'd say, "my ancestry goes back to Africa but I don't know what tribe it was." Invariably some would come up to me afterward and say, "Oh, you must have gotten your start with us. Your ancestors must have come from our tribe."

Telling them that this American black man got his start in Africa and that he was glad to be back in his beautiful motherland always thrilled them. It gave me a rapport that always brought spiritual results as well as love and affection.

I was invited into the African homes and ate African "chop" with them. In Lagos, Nigeria, I had my first bowl of their thick, thick peanut soup. You can tell Lagos is the peanut capital of Africa the moment you step off the plane. The smell of peanuts overwhelms you.

I also sang and gave a prayer of blessing at an African wedding. The ceremony was a cross between a coronation and a revival service. The elaborate African garb with emphasis on gold colors gave the wedding party an air of royalty. But the congregational singing, the solos, the many prayers and blessings and finally a communion service along with the exchange of vows would have made an old time Baptist feel right at home.

It was beautiful.

In fact, my whole African experience was beautiful: the correspondence with Dr. Edman, the travel to and across a beautiful and exciting continent, working under the banner of the Billy Graham Evangelistic Association, the acceptance, the love, the opportunities, the ministry which saw thousands of Africans brought into a personal relationship with Jesus Christ.

I was in fabled Africa representing the greatest evangelist since Dwight Moody and Billy Sunday. I was singing and speaking before greater crowds than I had ever dreamed of. I was seeing and doing and experiencing things as far removed from the gutter fights of San Francisco as could be imagined.

All of these would contribute to my growing self-confidence as well as a growing trust in the Lord of the harvest.

But Africa meant much more to me personally. It did for me what no amount of world travel, association with prominent persons or huge crowds could do.

It gave me an identity.

There was a time when I was ashamed to admit even to myself that my ancestors had come from Africa. Thanks to the comics and to Hollywood, I grew up with a mental picture of the African as a person with a ring in his nose, a bone in his hair and a spear in his hands. He was a naked savage swinging through trees in a Tarzan movie. He was a cannibal boiling a missionary in a newspaper cartoon.

We black Americans couldn't look back with pride to our ancestors. Furthermore we weren't accepted in the land of our birth. We didn't have much of a future to look forward to either.

We were burdened by a sense of shame, by a lack of identity. By futility.

Africa changed all this for me.

From the jungle clearing to the gleaming cities I found culture and dignity and respect on this beautiful continent. I had stepped back into my ancestral past and found it valid.

Of course I didn't miss the squalor and primitive and backward aspects of Africa that were in such contrast to the beauty. This did something for me, too.

I imagined myself growing up in a heathen tribe in

the jungles of Africa. I imagined it and for the first time I thanked God even for slavery. Something good really did come of it. Man's inhumanity to man was ugly, but God used it for good.

Had it not been for slavery, perhaps I would have grown up in one of these primitive areas. I would have had no opportunity for education, for developing my talents, for enjoying modern civilization. Perhaps if some of my ancestors had not been forced from Africa to live under the nightmarish whip of the shipmaster and to be sold and put to work on the plantations of the South, I would not have had the opportunity to know the Lord and return with the Gospel.

My heart is burdened for Africa and for the black Christian of America to reach it. I feel a sense of urgency. So many Africans are responsive to the American Negro evangel. If we blacks do not respond to this need we are going to miss perhaps the greatest opportunity we have ever had. The course of history is such that it is our hour to make a spiritual impact on Africa.

Our ancestors came over on slave ships. Now it is time for us to go back as slaves of Jesus so that, paradoxically, the black African might really be free.

I went to Africa and found acceptance and love and identity.

But it's more than that, man.

We're needed. Desperately needed.

There are multitudes of Africans who will never know our beautiful Savior unless we as a black church awake to these needs and send a host of our people to the Africa of our ancestry.

CHAPTER ELEVEN

With Billy Graham in Chicago

Commencement day, 1951, had been the beginning, all right. *The beginning of the end,* I had thought bitterly. I couldn't even join a little summer evangelistic team with Earl and Eddie because "we don't grant credentials to Negroes."

A little over a decade later, in February of 1962, I suddenly became an associate of Billy Graham. "What God has appointed, no man can take away," my mother had told me.

The invitation to join as a full member of the Graham team came as Howard Jones and I were still up to our elbows in ministry in Africa. We received a phone call and later more extensive contact by ham radio from the Graham Association. Their crusade in Chicago was about to begin and they wanted Howard and me back to be part of it.

The tide had completely turned. In 1951 I couldn't become a minister because I was black. In 1961 I was sent to Africa *because* I was black and in 1962 I was invited to join the Billy Graham team *because,* among other things, I was black.

From being a dead albatross around my neck, my black skin had suddenly become a soaring eagle. Instead of a wall to keep me out, it had become a pass to get me into the most coveted of inner circles.

Black indeed was becoming beautiful.

The cynical, of course, will say that Howard Jones and then myself and later other blacks were put on the Team as a token gesture. It just isn't true.

I learned this for myself when we were abruptly brought back from Africa to meet with Billy Graham in Denver where he was to be the key-note speaker at the National Association of Evangelicals Convention. Billy met with Howard and me for about forty-five minutes in his hotel suite.

He asked for a full report on our ministry in Africa and then counseled with us and unburdened his heart for Chicago. "I've been disappointed," he said, "that we've only received a small response from Negroes in our crusades. With you fellows on the team I'm praying that God will give us a real harvest among the black people."

Even though Graham was a product of the South, I had no doubts about his sincerity in reaching blacks for the Lord. In the years that would follow I saw the full evidence of his real love and concern for all minority peoples. His love for Jesus Christ is such that it overflows to all men whether they be in prison or in a gang, whether they are wealthy or destitute, or whether they are European or Asian, black or white.

I was drawn into the warmth of that love from this first encounter with Billy Graham, and all of my life since has felt the afterglow.

The cynical might also say that I was flaunting my blackness, parading the fact that I had become a member of the Team because I was black while others of equal or superior ability and ministry — who would have given their right arms to be with Billy — didn't make it.

For Marilyn and me it wasn't that kind of ball game. When Marilyn joined me for a few days in Chicago, it was with a feeling of great honor and awe that we were introduced to the board members and team members. But it was also with a great humility. God had allowed us, little nobodies from a small church in a dark corner of San Francisco, to be here rubbing shoulders with some of the greatest men in Christian circles.

With tears pouring down our cheeks, Marilyn and I praised God for the opportunity He had given us. We acknowledged that we didn't know how long our association with Billy would last, but we told the Lord that we wanted only His purpose and His glory.

Marilyn, who has always had a tremendous spiritual perception, felt that the Lord was giving us this opportunity for a special purpose.

"Bob, I believe God has placed you on the Graham team to prepare you for an even greater ministry," she told me.

At the time I couldn't imagine anything greater than being with Billy Graham. Time, I believe, has proved her right. I have had no greater honor in my life than being a member of his team, but I can see now that this really was a proving time. God was preparing me for a ministry where Billy himself was to say he could be of only limited effectiveness.

My church in San Francisco had graciously given me a leave of absence for the European trip and then the African trip. This time, however, I was accepting a paid staff position with Billy Graham for an indefinite period and I would have to leave the church. I knew I was doing what the Lord wanted and in a human sense I was stepping up. But it was nonetheless hard to say good-by to these dear people who had come to know the Lord under my first ministry and who had labored and loved in the process of building up their church.

It was going to be harder on the family. By now there were four Harrison kids: Keith, age 10, Carol, 8, Adrienne, 5, and little David, 3. The family would remain in San Francisco while I traveled all over the continent with the Graham team.

I had a twinge of worry in being gone from them so much. I remembered the problems I had in my home because dad wasn't there. In dad's case it was because we were poor and in my case it was because of an expanding ministry. But I was concerned that the ultimate effect might still be the same.

I vowed then to be as close to the family as I possibly could when I was at home.

The Chicago Crusade at McCormack Place began in all its grandeur. I was awestruck by the crowds of 50,000 and more. I couldn't believe what was happening to me. I only wished I was sharing my experiences with Earl and Eddie. We had counted so much on that first evangelistic team. My blackness had prevented it, and now my blackness had taken me where they probably would never go.

The mass meetings of the Billy Graham crusades are well-known to the Christian public. Being an official part of these was certainly exciting. On the platform I was involved in reading the Scripture and praying. Behind the scenes I was involved in such things as coordinating the counseling and follow-up, taking charge of advisors and counselors, watching for overflow crowds and so on.

One night in Chicago we had 50,000 jammed into McCormack Place and about 6,000 on the outside. We opened up an additional auditorium which seated 5,500 and held a simultaneous meeting.

I played for the entire service, sang, gave my testimony and then the late Dr. Joe Blinco gave the message. We had a tremendous response to the meeting with many coming forward to accept the Lord.

Of equal thrill to me was being a part of the inner workings of the Team: the press conferences, the private meetings with prominent figures, the Team prayer meetings and planning sessions, the ministers' meetings and radio and T.V. programs and the miscellaneous meetings that took us into schools, factories, service clubs, jails and every other place where people are gathered.

Billy wasn't involved in all of these, but one extra meeting in Chicago I'll never forget. Billy accepted the invitation to go to the south side of Chicago and meet with members of eighteen different gangs. He brought Howard and me with him to help provide a point of contact.

The event was written up in the local papers and later in the national news magazines. These gangs had been a center of national attention because of their many rumbles. The leader of a Puerto Rican gang came to know the Lord through Youth for Christ, however, and became concerned for his cohorts.

He arranged for Billy to come down to the area and then stayed up all night going into every dive and den to invite gang members to meet him.

When we were ushered into a dimly lit gang headquarters, there were about 150 to 200 toughs there. Some of their clothes were cut and bloody from fights just a few hours before.

We first wandered around the room, shaking hands and chatting with some of the guys. I used some of the vernacular I had learned on the streets of San Francisco and this helped establish some rapport. We were all very loose and free and easy. You couldn't very well be a stuffed-shirt in this crowd.

Billy was finally introduced formally and a hush fell over the guys. It was amazing to see the Holy Spirit move in and take charge.

"Hi, fellows," Billy said casually. "It's an honor to be here and it is great to take a little time to share some things with you."

He introduced me as one who grew up in Fillmore and had been an entertainer. They listened attentively to my songs and then my testimony.

I was impressed with the way Billy worked in this situation. He really knew how to reach these fellows. He started out with some jokes and got the fellows laughing. Then he skillfully worked into a message on the manliness of Jesus. He was hitting them where they lived.

After a final prayer, he invited these hoodlums to come to the crusade. "We would like you to be our honored guests," he said. "How many of you will come if we send a bus for you?"

There was a strained silence before a couple of hands finally went up. It was turning into an awkward situation, but our converted Puerto Rican gang leader came to the rescue.

"Hey, you guys, you know me, don't you?" he said, standing up.

They nodded their heads.

"I'm a right guy, ain't I?"

"Yea," they answered in chorus.

He reminded them of how he used to fight and how he had led his gang against many of them.

"Well," he said, "my friend Billy Graham is here and he is inviting you to McCormack Place. I'm saying you ought to go. Now let's see how many of you are going."

Hands started flying up all over the place.

The gangs filled two busses that night. They entered McCormack and did kind of a sharpie walk down the aisle to their front seats, all the time looking around as if they were casing the place. They were trying to act tough, but you could tell they were touched that someone as big as Billy Graham would honor them and acknowledge they were human after all.

At the invitation later, many came forward. A number gave their guns and knives to the counselors and walked away with Bibles. It was a beautiful sight to behold, and thrilling to be part of.

When we were invited on the team, Howard and I were assured that our ministries would not be just to the black community. We were not there just to be symbols or to be exploited.

They really kept their promise and our ministries took us everywhere. I was in many white churches and ministerial meetings and spoke at a number of the evangelical colleges in the area. These included Wheaton College, North Park College and Seminary, Trinity Evangelical Divinity School, Moody Bible Institute and a number of other schools well-known in the Midwest. This was my first exposure to these schools and my first knowledge of some of them.

But there was no question that our value to the team included getting the black churches involved. I therefore spoke and sang in a number of black churches in the Chicago area. One of my invitations was from Rev. Louis Boddie, pastor of Greater Harvest Baptist Church. This is one of the leading black churches in Chicago and Pastor Boddie had a tremendous influence on all the black community through an extensive radio ministry.

On a Sunday morning I spoke on the theme of all of us being members of the body of Christ. There was such an enthusiastic response I was invited to return on a Sunday evening for an evangelistic service. This time I spoke on the second coming. I later learned that this was the first message on the subject in this church. The pastor was floored as deacons, choir members and others who had been attending for years came forward to commit their lives to Christ. Many acknowledged that they wouldn't have been ready for the Lord at His return.

Rev. Boddie invited me to speak three different times on his radio broadcast so that I might have a ministry with many thousands more. Through the church and radio we started a drive to get blacks to attend the crusade.

The culmination came when about five hundred Negroes stood and were introduced to the crowd at the crusade one night. That represented only about one percent of the crowd in a city with a vast black population, but it was nevertheless a gratifying moment for me.

The Chicago crusade was a thrilling and satisfying adventure. Among other things, I was helping to bridge the gap between the black and white Christian and also helping to get the black church concerned about and involved in evangelism. It was just a beginning and there was a long way to go, but at least it *was* a beginning.

CHAPTER TWELVE

Five Fantastic Years

When the Chicago meetings were over, I flew to San Francisco to keep that pledge to the family and to share with Marilyn and the kids the excitement of my association with Billy Graham. In all, I was to spend five fantastic years with Graham during which time I would participate in six major crusades including Chicago, Fresno, Los Angeles, Omaha, Boston and Denver.

Chicago, like the first crack at any adventure, is etched in my mind in minute, scintillating detail. But in Fresno, just the second crusade, the seeds for my leaving the team were being planted, though I could not know it at the time.

Not all associates are involved in every crusade, and in the case of Fresno it was Larry Love and myself who arrived in town two months ahead of time to begin pre-crusade activity.

We chased all over town to meet with the press, to speak at service clubs, business groups, churches, ministers' meetings, pre-crusade rallies, and to appear on radio and T.V. programs.

The fact that I was one of just two representatives in town in the early stages of the preparation coupled with the fact of a large black community in Fresno was to provide a real test case in getting Negro involvement in a crusade. Knowing how my black brothers love to sing, I implored the music directors to get their people to join the 1,000-voice crusade choir. I also turned on all the enthusiasm and personality I could muster to get church members to attend the crusade with their unconverted friends. I vigorously promoted the counselor training courses as well.

The result of all this effort was somewhat disappointing. Quite a few attended the crusade and we had some success in getting black choir members. But in both cases it was a relatively small percent of the black Christian community.

We especially drooped when we saw the very limited response to our drive to get black counselors. This made it difficult when blacks came forward and we had no black counselors to meet them. The Graham team works hard in trying to pair every person responding to the invitation with an appropriate counselor. This is done by age, by sex and by interest.

This didn't necessarily mean that every Negro had to be counseled by another Negro or that we wanted a Negro convert to attend a Negro church. But in an area such as Fresno, with a large black community, it just didn't look good to have so few blacks counseling. The blacks attending couldn't help wondering what was wrong with the organization and with evangelical Christianity that it was so lily-white.

I can't entirely blame the Negro Christians for their weak showing. The Negro is basically still very suspicious of most evangelicals because he equates them with bigotry and prejudice. He is painfully aware that few blacks have been welcome in white evangelical churches and schools and camps and other functions.

The hurt in the Negro Christian runs deep, and he's not about to expose himself to the possibility of further abuse. He must have many, many good experiences before he will believe that they are the norm and the bad experiences the exception.

For my part, then, I felt not only a keen responsibility to challenge blacks but to expose whites to the Negro Christian and church. Being on the Graham team provided many opportunities for this. Just my black presence, without preaching on the topic at all, provided a bridge of understanding.

During the Omaha crusade in 1964, for instance, I was invited by the people of Central City, some seventy miles distance, to conduct a crusade. They realized their town was too small for Billy to come for a full crusade, but they were turned on by what they saw in Omaha and wanted to reach their own city for Christ.

The invitation was channeled through the Association office and I went there for a four-night crusade after Omaha was finished. We had about 1600 attending nightly, which was a good percentage of the population. Many came to know the Lord.

Like so many evangelicals, these Christians simply didn't know any Negroes. There were none in the town. I became the first black to speak in their high school, in many of the civic and service groups, and certainly the first to hold a nightly crusade.

They didn't know what to expect from a black and they were watching me closely. Much to their surprise, they found that Negroes were just people not significantly different from the people they knew in their own circles.

By being black and by being a co-worker of Billy Graham, I was in a position to help bridge the gap between the black and white Christian. But it was never enough. Time would come when both Billy and I would realize that I could actually be more effective off the team.

In the meantime, I grew and matured in the close association of this great man of God.

Much has been written about Billy Graham the great evangelist, Billy Graham the world citizen, Billy Graham the outstanding personality, but I haven't read anything that speaks about the relationship Billy has with his immediate team members.

I think the first thing that impressed me was the closeness of the team itself. There seemed to be a feeling of dependency upon one another, a spiritual dependency, a dependency for fellowship and encouragement.

Any time I was facing a problem, I felt I could go to any of the team members and be assured they would pick up the burden of the problem with me.

All this was undoubtedly because Billy himself set the precedent with his own devotion and love for his Lord and love for us.

The high point of my experience with Graham was always the team meetings which took place with every crusade. Billy would call us together, usually in the morning. After breakfast together, we would have a time of fellowship and a time of self-searching to make certain there was nothing to hinder the free flow of the Spirit through us.

Billy always set the stage for this. He would call us to a time of prayer. It was a time when we didn't just recite prayers, but we would spend an hour or an hour and a half, sometimes two hours pouring out our hearts to God. Each of us would pray but it wouldn't necessarily follow a particular order. If I felt led to pray I would and then someone would follow after me. If

I felt like praying a second or third time during these rich experiences, I would.

There were times when many of us would be broken, weeping before God as we sought God's will and purpose for the ministry of the Billy Graham Association or for a particular city.

At the close of prayer Billy would share from the Word with us. He would speak from his heart as one man to another. He was like an elder brother to all of us.

After the devotional time, we sometimes would go back to prayer again. On occasion, these sessions would go on for two, three or four hours.

Billy's devotion and spirit was contagious, causing us to search for that place of ultimate dedication and devotion.

This undoubtedly is one of the prime reasons why the Graham team has held together over such a long period of time. This is why I found no discord, no argument, no serious disagreement during the whole time I was with them.

The harmony of the team also results from Billy's personality. It's almost unbelievable how unassuming and relaxed a person he is.

As busy as Billy always was with his heavy schedule, he frequently took time for personal counseling and a personal time of prayer with individual members.

I remember several times when just Billy and I talked together. He counseled with me, and he shared some of his experiences with me. No matter what we talked about, though, it always ended up on a spiritual note and a time of prayer.

All of this obviously made a tremendous impact upon my life and my future ministry. Even now there are times when I become a little discouraged and I think back to the encouraging remarks Billy made. It's always a tremendous boost to me. To remember this giant of a figure, used by God in such a tremendous way, taking time to speak with me and to pray with me means so very much.

Billy occasionally would refer to his experience at Forest Home just before the 1949 crusade in Los Angeles. He was having a good ministry, but he was driven to his knees because he felt something was missing.

He prayed and prayed and waited upon God. He described for us the wonderful experience of being filled with the Holy Spirit, and how his ministry changed from that time.

I've participated with Billy in many ministers' meetings where twelve hundred to eighteen hundred pastors were gathered. Almost always his subject to these spiritual leaders of God's people is the need for seeking the infilling of the Holy Spirit, the need for an anointed ministry, the need for a preaching from an overflow of the Spirit of God.

He asks the preachers why there is such powerlessness in multitudes of churches. His answer is that so often the ministers are not under the unction of the Holy Spirit.

Billy always emphasized this same filling of the Spirit with the team as well. He knows his effectiveness is only from the power of the Holy Spirit working in and through him.

You can perhaps imagine what an impact this made on my young life. I saw what God the Holy Spirit did through Billy, and I was excited at the prospect of what God the Holy Spirit could do through me. I found myself many times waiting upon God and asking to be filled and refilled time and time again, with the Holy Spirit and with the anointing.

One conversation with Billy while we were in Fresno

especially stands out in my mind. Cliff Barrows called my hotel room one afternoon and said Billy would like to see me and spend some time with me.

I went to his room and found out it was to be just a personal conversation between Billy and myself. We strolled through the normal courtesies of "how are you" and "how are things going?" He asked how I felt the crusade was going and how I was enjoying my relationship with the Graham team.

Then he zeroed in on the point of the meeting. He shared with me how God had impressed him with the musical and speaking talent God had given me. He emphasized and reemphasized the importance of making certain that I remained humble before the Lord.

"You must realize that everything you have, God has given you. No matter how people might applaud your musical talent or your speaking ability, you must always give the glory to God because God will not share His glory with another.

"As long as you remain humble, God will always use you. I feel that God has a great ministry for your life and this is just the beginning."

Then he said, "Bob, I think we should just spend some time in prayer right at this moment."

I led in a few moments of prayer and then Billy spent about ten minutes praying. He prayed for our ministry together, he prayed for the crusade, and then he prayed for me specifically. He asked that the Lord would always keep His hand on me, that I would always remain in the place where I would know the anointing of God, that I would stay humble before God so I could be used of Him.

How could my life go unchanged after a session like that?

During the Omaha Crusade, Billy and I were talking together again. At this time, racial strife was the number one topic in the nation. The need for more black voices in the field of evangelism weighed heavy upon me.

I shared this with Billy and he said he felt the same way. "Bob," he said, and I will never forget this, "you know you have an advantage over me, and that is the color of your skin. Because of the nationalism all around the world as well as black nationalism here, your skin can be a real passport for you. I believe under God that you can have a tremendous ministry, in some quarters a greater ministry than any white person." And then he repeated the words he had said to me before: "Bob, I believe if you remain humble and stay in the place of dedication, God can use you as a black voice to call people to the foot of the cross and also give a sense of direction regarding this terrible problem that is perplexing all of us."

I stayed with Graham through two more crusades (Boston and Denver), but the feeling grew in me that the time had come for the "greater ministry" Marilyn had believed in.

So by mutual consent, and certainly under the leading of Almighty God, those five fantastic years with Billy Graham came to an end.

The end for me, however, was like the end of school. It was graduation, it was commencement, it was the beginning of a whole new outreach in ministry into which God would lead me.

CHAPTER THIRTEEN

Joseph in Egypt

I owe so much to Billy and his board and associates for their courage and foresight in making me part of the team. From obscurity, they gave me a platform so this black voice ultimately could be heard all over America and on every continent in the world. They gave me training and experience and made a spiritual impact on my life which was priceless. By the time God would lead us to the parting of our ways, they had prepared me for a ministry that would be uniquely my own.

Indirectly, they were even responsible for my finally becoming an ordained minister and thereby breaking down the "white only" barriers of a major denomination.

Eleven years had passed since the Friday afternoon when the sky fell. In the intervening years I had been a pastor, an evangelist in Europe and Africa, and finally a member of the Billy Graham team.

All this without ever being ordained.

I didn't make an issue of the matter. When the door was slammed in my face I didn't try to break it open.

I can't say I really listened to my mother, either. She

would always see the silver lining in the dark cloud. Her blackness made her identify with such Bible characters as Joseph. But it wasn't the bitterness of the persecution and hatred toward Joseph that impressed her so much as the ultimate victory he found as the king's right hand man in Egypt.

"The very ones who are putting you down,'" she said during those dark days after Bible school graduation, "will someday be the ones who will honor you."

It didn't turn out to be the men involved — some of them had died or had left positions of authority in the meantime — but it did turn out to be their successors in the same positions.

The injustice of my case smoldered in the hearts and minds of my school buddies and friends among faculty members and pastors in the denomination. Five years later at the national convention in Springfield, Missouri, attended by some 3,000 Assemblies of God delegates, the embers were fanned into flame. The case of Bob Harrison, first Negro ever to apply for credentials in the denomination, was brought to the floor. After an impassioned debate, the problem of what to do about blacks applying for credentials was given a half solution — the kind that committees everywhere are so disposed to. It was decided that the granting of a license to preach was a district function and that the national body could not dictate this policy.

With this decision, a black could now be granted a license from his district, if it so approved, but he still could not be granted ordination. This was to remain a function of the national office.

The war hadn't been won, but victory had been achieved in a major battle.

I was invited to the next district meeting in Santa Cruz. The superintendent who had presided over my application refusal was dead and along with him had died the southern prejudices of his upbringing. A younger man more liberal in his thinking in these matters — and a personal friend of mine — had taken his place.

"Bob," he said, "what happened to you was totally unjust and we are making many efforts to correct the situation. I really think changes are going to be made."

What he was saying amounted to this: Would I give them another chance?

In just a matter of a few months word came from this new superintendent. He asked me to come down and make another application for license, which I did.

The license was granted, the first to a Negro in this 600,000-member denomination. But it had come five years too late for me to be jubilant. Why did the incidental shade of my skin have to degrade me so? Why could I be licensed but not ordained? Would God ever get out of the ghetto?

Several more years passed and brought me ultimately to the Graham team in Chicago. One night the General Superintendent of the Assemblies along with the man who had become president of Bethany Bible College attended the crusade and Billy invited them to be his guests on the platform.

When they saw me there they turned handsprings. They shook hands, they hugged me, they slapped me on the back.

"We're so proud to have our boy on the Billy Graham team," they chorused.

"The very ones," my mother had said.

When I was a Negro from the Fillmore area of San Francisco I wasn't good enough to become one of "their boys." But the magic name of Billy Graham was so dazzling it was harder to see the black skin and suddenly it was "our boy."

This was but the beginning. Two days later I received a phone call from the denomination headquarters in Springfield, Missouri.

The payoff was that they were inviting me down to visit their headquarters at their expense.

Five days later I flew down and met many of the officials of the denomination. They gave me a grand tour of their magnificent headquarters buildings. I think they were trying to impress me. "You are with the great Billy Graham organization, but we are a big outfit, too," they seemed to be saying.

I learned that the Assemblies was one of the fastest growing denominations in the world (they were eighth largest), they had more Bible schools than anyone else (nine), they had two liberal arts schools and they gave more to the N.A.E. than any other denomination. I learned of their world-wide outreach (which was impressive) and especially of their work in Brazil where they are the largest Protestant denomination.

After the tour I was given a private audience with the head of the missions department.

"You can write your own ticket, Bob, if you'll come and minister under our banner," he said.

He promised an extensive expense account, travel to Africa, the Caribbean, the Fiji islands and other exotic places. (I noticed that the places mentioned all had the common denominator of having a large black population. It wasn't hard to see the line of their thinking.)

As gently as possible I gave the knife just a little twist.

"This all sounds great," I said, "but how can it be possible when I don't even carry ordination papers with the denomination?"

He inferred that this might be arranged if I would just come with the organization.

I had to savor this beautiful scene for a while.

"Well, I'll see," I said. "Right now I'm pretty tied up with Graham. I'll let you know."

Humanly, I wanted to mock the hypocrisy of the denomination that had excluded Negroes for generations only to change their minds when public opinion was changing and when they found a black who was "not like the rest." Why isn't the Church of Jesus Christ ahead of the world in matters like this instead of dragging behind? Why aren't matters decided by what is right and true and not by expediency?

In my heart, however, I knew these men were human, too, and that they were sincere. Also, I couldn't lay sixty years of sin of a whole denomination on their backs.

The Assemblies did even better than their word. Without my leaving the Graham team they granted my ordination. It was between the Chicago and Fresno Crusades when I was briefly in San Francisco that I received a call from the Northern California-Nevada District Superintendent. He said that he had received an okay concerning my ordination and asked when I could come to Santa Cruz to accept it. Even at that time, between crusades, I had a heavy schedule, but I was able to block off a couple of hours a week later when I was to be in the area.

It was a different scene when I was ushered into the presence of the district presbytery than it had been in this same city eleven years earlier. There were congratulations and expressions of how proud they were of my ministry and of my being a product of their school.

They laid their hands on me, had a prayer of dedication, and handed me the ordination papers.

"The very ones . . . ."

It was an emotional moment for me.

It was no longer so important that I was being ordained. After all, I had been a pastor and had ministered on two continents besides the United States, and I was an associate of Billy Graham. But I could see my mother waiting in the car for me those eleven years before, expecting that I could walk into the committee and be ordained like anyone else.

I could see a whole new day dawning for the black Christians of America. The tears, the frustrations, the humiliations were all worth it. One Negro being ordained in a major denomination would certainly mean that many more would follow. It would mean that many other denominations with a Jim Crow clergy would be challenged to change.

I could look further into the future and see black men, proud and erect and purposeful, becoming heroes of the cross all over America and around the globe. I could see that when God was black He was just as beautiful and powerful as when He was white.

It was a beautiful moment.

Since that day in 1962 the Assemblies of God have continued to take important strides in reaching and accepting the black man they had shunned. They have opened black churches, they have given scholarships to top black students, they have included black history in their Sunday school material and they have met in top level conferences which included black leaders where they really come to grips with the challenge of the black community.

To date, this has all resulted in twenty-five more blacks being ordained and placed in the ministry. The results have been well worth the humiliations I had to experience as the vanguard of this force. I pray that this denomination will increasingly become a haven where black Christians will be welcomed and be able to get the training and experience and acceptance necessary to become the vital force in world evangelism that the Lord certainly has ordained for us.

Ironically, of course, main-line denominations — Episcopal, Methodist, Congregational, Presbyterian, etc., have been ordaining blacks for years. Why have some denominations been so slow?

CHAPTER FOURTEEN

How It Could Have Been

I've been saying all along that black Christians represent a vast potential for effective service in worldwide evangelism and missions. Maybe *you're* saying it just isn't so.

Negroes are too lazy. If they had any potential they would have accomplished something by now.

And black churches are too liberal. They're interested in social justice and economic improvements and not evangelism and missions.

I'm going to skip over that first one. If you still believe that cliché, I'm probably not going to impress you with what I might say to the contrary.

The second one needs some attention, however, because a vast majority of the ten million black church members *do* attend churches with a liberal orientation.

How did that happen?

It happened while forty million white evangelicals were making themselves comfortable behind the stained glass of their all-white segregated churches.

Black Christians were weak when they could have

been strong, but this was at least partly because white Christians found it less unsettling to their nerves to be concerned with correct doctrine and keeping themselves "separated from the world."

They were separated from the world, all right – the world of hopelessness and frustration, the world of malnutrition and menial jobs, the world of blackness and segregation.

The liberal church, however patronizing and paternalistic it was, paid attention. They saw discrimination, they saw poverty, they saw joblessness and hopelessness and did something about it.

They sympathized and they helped. They took blacks into their schools and into their churches and the black church appreciated it.

They came with a social gospel, but at least they came. The fundamental churches ridiculed the liberal's social consciousness but came with *no* gospel.

So the black church, by and large, became liberal.

But the word "liberal" needs some explanation when applied to the black church. They are liberal in the sense of their identification with the liberal church of America and they are liberal politically to a large extent. If you were a victim of the social patterns of the day, you would not want to conserve them either. You would be clamoring for change. You would be a liberal.

This liberalness, however, did not result in a great black turning to liberal *theology.*

I know of few black churches anywhere that deny such basic Bible doctrines as the deity of Christ, the virgin birth, the miracles, the resurrection of Jesus and the inspiration and authority of the Scriptures.

Martin Luther King, Jr., for instance, was surely a liberal in the political sense. But he never denied any of the basic doctrines of evangelicalism.

Black church members believe the Bible. The great tragedy is that they are untaught in the Scriptures. They haven't rejected them, they just don't know too much of what they say. Because of the influence of the liberals they see the social implications of the Gospel but not always the personal implications in commitment to Jesus Christ.

While the black church continued in its paradoxical belief and ignorance, the white evangelical churches, ever the purists, from their lofty pinnacles of correct theology took careful note and condemned black liberalism. They analyzed and criticized and thereby excused themselves from doing anything.

How different it could have been.

I don't think I fully appreciated what the black church might have become had the circumstances been different until the day I visited Forest Home Conference Grounds in the San Bernadino Mountains of southern California.

I was at the Los Angeles crusade in 1964 and inundated in the usual round of luncheons, press conferences and miscellaneous meetings. I was beat. Driving seventy miles to Forest Home to sing and speak and then return in time for the evening crusade meeting didn't appeal to me. I tried to cancel, but my coming had been publicized so widely that canceling would have been embarrassing to the conference and to the Graham Association.

When I arrived I was amazed at the size of Forest Home. The facilities are tremendous. Then, as I was introduced around, I was flabbergasted at the size of the staff and the extent of the program.

They briefed me on my activities and eventually took me to Hormel Auditorium. Nine hundred high school kids were jammed into this hall. Every seat was

When God Was Black

filled and they were standing in the doorways and along the edges of the room.

By the time I was introduced the adrenalin was coursing madly through my veins. I sat down at the piano mike and cracked a few jokes.

"Though there isn't any television here," I said, "I think you can see that I'm coming through in living color. Before today, I've always believed in integration — that's why I play on both the black notes and the white notes. After meeting your camp director, however, I might have to change my mind."

I went on like that and these energetic teenagers roared their approval.

I belted out "Down by the Riverside," the "Amen Chorus" and a few others with real rhythm. I nodded my head and tapped my foot in tempo and the kids picked up the beat by clapping their hands. They were really with me.

Then I eased into my message, a combination of my own testimony and a portrayal of what it really meant to be committed to Christ.

An unusual anointing and deep burden came upon me as I was ministering to these kids. I sensed that God was speaking directly to many. Looking over that large group of teenagers who had been laughing and clapping a few minutes before, I saw tears glistening in many eyes.

At the end I gave an invitation for those who had never commited their lives to Jesus Christ to come forward and do so. Again I was shocked and amazed. I had assumed that at this evangelical camp most of the kids would be sharp Christians from strong churches.

But in the crowd of 900, more than a third came forward at this invitation.

I gave a second invitation for those who would like

to surrender their lives to full-time Christian service and more came forward.

The counselors were busy the rest of the day, leading those sincere kids into new relationships with the Savior.

The meeting had begun at 10:30 A.M., but at well past five I was still counseling with individual kids and with groups of kids. Finally I had to break away and make a mad dash for the meeting in L.A.

Just one day at Forest Home and I could immediately see why the white church of North America had 28,000 foreign missionaries overseas and was turning out hundreds of pastors, ministers of Christian education and youth directors every year.

Each summer, all over America, tens of thousands of white young people were spending whole weeks under this kind of intensive training and challenge from the great men of God of our day.

Twenty-four hours a day for six or seven days their minds and hearts were being permeated with teachings of the Savior. Thousands of trained counselors were helping each of these individuals lock step with the Lord.

The needs of the uncommitted of America and of the world were being dramatically brought to these idealistic young whites who were searching for a cause to champion.

Many of these kids, I learned, would return year after year beginning with the junior camp and going on up through the college briefing conference. As the challenge of one summer began to grow cold, another summer came along and line was added to line and precept to precept. The impact of the previous summer was compounded by the impact of this summer.

I learned that about 34,000 had attended this one camp alone in this one year and that there are dozens of similar camps for evangelicals around the country.

White evangelicals, that is.

In that sea of 900 bubbling young faces there was nary a dark one. The next year I returned to Forest Home to participate in their family group. I brought my family, too, and in so doing I brought the first black young people ever to attend any of their regular conferences, I was told.

As for me, I was already in my thirties and an established singer and musician and associate of the greatest evangelist of our time before I attended my first interdenominational camp. (I had gone to a little denominational camp once as a boy.)

Are you still wondering why our black churches aren't turning out strong evangelical leaders and leading millions of black church members into Christian battlefields around the globe to win victories for Jesus Christ?

Where will our young people exchange their inherited, second generation religion for a deep personal experience with Jesus Christ?

Not in most of our black churches. We were in need and the liberal church came and helped and led us into a shallow, ethical, social religion.

Not in the great conference centers of the nation where tens of thousands of white kids learn Christ. We've been excluded.

Not in the mighty evangelical schools of the country. The token integration of a few of the "right kind" of Negroes has left the rest of the thousands of qualified ones out.

To write us off as being too liberal or too lazy is to throw out valuable ore because of all the dirt. There is a rich vein to be mined among the ten million believing but untaught Negro church members. The evangelical conference centers, Bible schools and colleges, mission societies and hundreds of other organizations and, yes, the evangelical churches can become the smelter for purifying and getting the value out of the black church. But they can do nothing until the ore is allowed into the receptacle.

But I am encouraged.

I *am* a Negro and I *was* at the camp and I did make my presence felt. That one meeting, surely ordained of God, was so unusual and so anointed by the Holy Spirit that it paved the way for my return to Forest Home for the next four years in various conferences and capacities. On each of these occasions I requested that my whole family be allowed to come. To their credit, the Forest Home people eagerly agreed. This meant that for the first time several of the children's youth camps were being integrated.

This first experience of mine in an interdenominational conference center opened doors to other camps and I have now participated in conferences at Hume Lake and Mt. Hermon in California and the Firs in Washington.

In each case these camps were going through their first or one of their first experiences with Negroes participating and taking leadership. I and my family were test cases. They wanted to see how we would fit in, how we would be accepted, what kind of an attitude we had, what kind of ministry I would have.

With my dramatic first experience, these questions were soon resolved. Now they wanted to know if I was typical or a special case. In my second visit to Forest Home I met with some of the staff members in an informal session to talk about the racial problem. It was an impromptu session, but we ended up spending almost three hours on the subject.

We talked about the need for opening up the conference grounds to all Negroes, for informing Negroes that they were welcome, and promoting and in some cases even subsidizing their attendance.

The possibility of bringing blacks on the grounds brought up a whole kettle full of questions which I tried to answer. They wanted to know how to treat Negroes, what to say and what to do.

I told them they had to learn to think black. Our culture, our thought patterns, our frame of reference is different from the white man's. I encouraged them to take the time and make the effort to learn the culture even as a foreign missionary does or a Young Life leader does when he goes on a strange campus.

We went into all the problems of how to gain rapport with blacks and how to deal with those who had chips on their shoulders.

I talked about how our girls need to treat their hair with hot irons because of the coarseness of their hair (this was before the "Afro" became popular) and about their special hygiene and dress problems. We talked about black and white boy-girl relationships and just about every aspect of the problem.

I emphasized the point that the blacks had not only something to gain but something to give. The part of God that was black was as vital to the whole as was any other part. For if tens of thousands of blacks had had these same summer experiences year after year, who can say what great advances would have been made in foreign missions, in revival and evangelism in black churches and perhaps even in a greatly changed complexion of the whole scene in America?

The church and the pastor are still the heart of all the social and political as well as religious life of the American black.

What if these millions of blacks in thousands of churches had been really included in the training and zeal of the white evangelical church? Would not America of the sixties and even much of the world have been quite different?

That first experience at Forest Home gave me a glimpse of what it could have been like for the black church. But the walls are beginning to vibrate and the time will come when they will crumble and fall.

My vision of how it could have been is now turning to what it might yet become.

CHAPTER FIFTEEN

What Do Blacks Really Want?

Over and over again white America asks this question in exasperation: "What do blacks really want? They have a higher percentage of college grads than do the people of England, they have more cars per capita than the people of any other nation, they have laws that give them equal voting and work rights. And they only get more surly and demanding. What do they really want?"

When I walked into the office of Dr. Dick Hillis of Overseas Crusades, Incorporated, one day in August of 1965, I got what blacks really want.

I had first met Dick Hillis in Fresno, California, at a ministers meeting held in connection with the Billy Graham crusade there. I had heard of the organization — Overseas Crusades — which he had founded and had read many of his books. I also knew of his warm relationship with Graham and that O.C. helped in the coordination of the Graham crusades overseas.

It was a pleasure to meet Dr. Hillis, though I can't

say that any bells rang or lights flashed, signaling the future significance of this introduction.

Months later I met Norm Nelson, the great "Singing Ambassador" of Overseas Crusades. He had ministered in the Orient for many years and his enthusiasm for the kind of ministry I could have in the Philippines and other countries of Asia got to me.

By this time I was on my own and was still casting about for the right way to develop my ministry.

I couldn't get Norm's idea out of my mind. About three weeks later I called Dick Hillis and made an appointment to see him in Palo Alto.

I was surprised with the modest office that Overseas Crusades had in what had been a funeral home in Palo Alto, California. The mission staff explained to me how they went to great lengths to keep the overhead as low as possible in the States so that most of the money could get into the actual ministry overseas.

This really impressed me. Here was an organization that was more interested in the ministry than the administrative and public relations aspects. I had seen many of the other kind.

Dick met me in his office not as the General Director of Overseas Crusades, or as one of the great voices among evangelical circles, or as Dick Hillis the author. He simply greeted me as Dick Hillis, my brother. He gave me a warm handshake and clapped me on the shoulder. This indicated to me that we were just brothers sitting down to talk man to man.

Here was a great man of God. Yet he was humble, too. He didn't try to sell me a bill of goods about O.C. or impress me with what they were doing.

We talked about the racial problems of our country and I saw that he was a sensitive man. He was concerned about the struggle of the black man in America and expressed his sorrow that the church of Jesus Christ had left it up to the government to handle the situation.

We talked about my activities with Billy and what I had been doing since I left the team.

"Bob," he said, "I really believe that a man of color can have a tremendous ministry in Asia. Have you ever given it any thought?"

I told him that Norm Nelson had planted the idea in my head some weeks before.

"Could O.C. coordinate a ministry of mine in Asia if I should go?" I asked Dick.

A smile lighted his face as he said, "Look, Bob, that's what O.C. is all about."

He took me to a map on his wall and showed me the areas of Asia where city-wide crusades might be set up for me. We had prayer together and began to put in motion the machinery that would ultimately take me for the first time to Asia.

What impressed me about this visit with Dick Hillis was that he had accepted me for my real worth. He wasn't pushing integration as a cause or trying to make his organization look good by having a showcase Negro. I didn't at all get the feeling from Dick that he thought I was a commodity which he could exploit or I provided an opportunity for him to demonstrate his charity. I was of value not because I was a Negro or in spite of being a Negro, but simply because of what I was as a Christian and a man.

He had a tremendous burden for the peoples of the world. He saw my specific talents and concern and realized how this could be used in world evangelism.

This is what the black of America really wants — to be accepted for his actual value. The black man wants and needs a job like everyone else, of course. But he wants to be given the job not because someone is being kind to him or as a handout but because he has something to contribute. This is what gives him a sense of dignity — a sense of worth as a human being.

This is why the whites of America can give and give and give to the black and still not have him satisfied. What he really wants and needs is not charity but acceptance.

After several more meetings with Dr. Hillis we agreed that I would go to Asia for about two months. He felt that it would be great to have a mixed team which would really portray Christianity and brotherly love. So it was decided that Norm Nelson would travel with me. Norm would prepare the hearts of the people with his powerful tenor voice and I would do the preaching and perhaps sing a song or two.

After much prayer, much preparation and a whole lot of fund raising, Norm and I left for the Orient in December of 1965 and stayed until the first part of February the next year.

Mercifully, the meetings we thought were arranged for us in Tokyo, our first stop, had not materialized and we were able to take a few days to get body and soul back together before embarking on this whirlwind tour.

In Formosa and then the Philippines we plunged into our schedule of meetings in schools and universities and indoor and outdoor crusades. In one unbelievable experience in a section of Manila known as Plaza Miranda, we saw crowds of as many as 20,000 miraculously gather from the streets and shops of this gay heart of the city.

In Dalat, Viet Nam, we were warmed and humbled as we ministered to Montagnard tribal people whose heroic spirit in serving the Lord in spite of tremendous persecution and death I had read about in the book, *Bamboo Cross*. As we visited military hospitals in Vietnam we were saddened and at the same time overwhelmed at the courage of American and Vietnamese servicemen whose bodies had been mangled and burned by war. We were no less stirred when fifteen Viet Cong prisoners of war stood to receive Christ in front of about 150 of their communist inmates in still another meeting.

Our crusade in Hue, the old imperial capital of French Indo-China, was particularly poignant. We were the last ones to make an evangelistic impact on a city-wide level before the infamous Tet offensive of 1967, a year after our visit. When we left the city, tanks that would defend the city were already rolling in.

We arrived in Singapore during the Chinese new year festivities and many pastors felt we would have trouble filling the 4,000 seat Union Hall where the crusade was to be held. Much to our astonishment, the first night the auditorium was three-fourths filled, the second night it was comfortably filled and the third and fourth nights crowds had to be turned away and the fire department had to close the doors. At each invitation, the altar was jammed — mostly with young people.

Besides these regular meetings in each country, of course, we had school meetings, service club meetings, breakfast meetings, press conferences and T.V. and radio dates. It was a terribly exhausting but nevertheless thrilling tour. It was my first opportunity to minister in Asia and I found as I had in every other place that thousands and thousands of people were responding to the gospel message through the preaching and singing of a black man and — in this case — his white companion.

Many felt that my approach would receive little public response from the more conservative and stoic Chinese. But one Chinese leader said, "This is our first Negro evangelist in the 103-year history of our church. We so much appreciate his renditions of the Negro spirituals which spoke to our hearts. The suffering and disappointments that his people suffered in the past are similar to our experiences and this made him able to communicate so effectively to our people."

Another Chinese pastor said, "This is the best crusade we have had since John Sung's meetings in the 1930's."

This comment, which I was to hear many times while ministering in the Orient, was especially significant, I thought. John Sung was the famous Chinese who earned his doctorate in engineering in the States. On his return ocean voyage he yielded to God's call to be an evangelist and literally threw his degree overboard. In the years that followed he rocked all of China and several other Asian countries with his evangelistic preaching. For this black preacher to be compared to him spoke volumes on the subject of the people of my race being effective vessels of God in the Orient.

In this the first such ministry of a black that I know of in Asia, Chinese, Indians, Malaysians, Filipinos, Vietnamese, tribal peoples, communists and American servicemen were hearing the Gospel for the first time — and some for the last. All of this came simply because one mission head was brave enough to give this black man what he really wanted — a chance to be accepted for what he was as a servant of Jesus Christ. If more evangelicals in the right places will give the black Christian "what he wants," who can tell what impact will be made on this ravaged globe of ours?

CHAPTER SIXTEEN

Who, Me, Lord?

Of the 28,000 missionaries sent out from America, I have been able to find only about a dozen or so who are black. Through my overseas adventures and experiences at home, the conviction was welling up within me that we could do much better than that. When God was black He could speak to brown hearts and black hearts and white hearts just as effectively as He could when He was white.

I had seen it and I had believed it and now I was ready to challenge *someone else* to go. Some pretty forceful messages were developing in my mind to deliver to my black brothers in Christ. I wanted them to send out missionaries. If one in a thousand black Christians went overseas, I reasoned, we would have a missionary force of 10,000.

Little did I know that God had a cute trick up His omnipresent sleeve. Before I was going to get an opportunity to give this challenge to our black churches, and before I would get a chance to see someone else sent out, God was going to send me and my family to the mission field.

On my return to the States in February of 1966 I had some miscellaneous meetings, a ten-day crusade in Barbados, West Indies, and then went to Mt. Hermon, California, to take part in the Overseas Crusades missionary conference in July. Naturally, a warm spot had developed in my heart for O.C. and I began to wonder if God was leading us into some closer relationship.

At the Mt. Hermon conference I gave reports on the experiences Norm and I had known in Asia. I also did some singing and playing.

Dick Hillis asked me to meet with the board of O.C., which convened during the conference. We came to pretty quick agreement that I should become one of their associate missionaries. This would mean further trips under the auspices of Overseas Crusades to various parts of the world where they ministered.

Specifically, definite plans began to take shape for an extended tour of South America in the first part of 1967.

It came as a bit of a surprise to me, then, when Dr. Hillis called me a couple of months later asking me to consider moving to the Philippines with my family.

"Bob," he said, "I just had a letter from Basil Costerisan in Manila. Our missionaries out there are asking you to consider coming to the Philippines for a year."

"But Dick, you know Norm and I have plans to go to South America in a few months," I said.

"I know that," said Dick. "But I think you ought to give serious consideration to this invitation. I want you to pray about it."

The logic wasn't there, and Dick, uncharacteristically, wasn't very convincing. But I agreed to pray. About three and a half weeks later I had another call from Dick. I told him that we still didn't feel strongly that we ought to go to Manila.

"Bob, I really feel that this is of the Lord," he said. I again said I'd spend some time in prayer, but I'm not sure my heart was in it.

I met with Dick sometime later and this time he laid it on the line. "You know, Bob," he said, "you have told me that one of your burdens is to see the field of foreign missions opened to the Negro. You've convinced me that this is one area where the Negro has not had opportunity to serve. I believe God is saying something to us now. Are you willing to let God make you the first black missionary O.C. has had and possibly one of the first with an evangelical organization?"

Now he was getting to me where I lived.

But there were still some pretty strong resistance factors in my life. One of them, of course, was South America. I had enjoyed traveling with Norm Nelson and was anticipating the ministry with him. The challenge and opportunities down there seemed so great.

There was undoubtedly the human element as well. By now this little black boy from the streets of Fillmore had preached and sung on every continent in the world with the exception of South America and Australia.

There were some other personal factors. Marilyn and I had come a long way from the ugly tenement housing projects of those first years as a struggling pastor. In the years following the Lord had kept every promise. He had supplied every need. With all that we had we sought first the Kingdom of God and He added all the other things unto us.

When I went with the Graham team my salary was such that I could devote my full energies to the ministry. For the first time I didn't have to worry about the necessities of life such as where the next pair of shoes for our growing children would come from.

Being with Graham had also launched me into a recording ministry. I was with Billy in the L.A. crusade when George Parsons, who took care of the literature distribution for the Team, convinced me that I ought to start making records. "I don't know why you haven't made a record before now," he said. He pushed me and cajoled me and finally we got my first L.P. together

Since then I have recorded a total of four L.P.'s and one 45 that have sold pretty well. My position with the Team also brought in concert engagements and opportunities to write for various periodicals. These also increased my income a little.

We were able to buy that nice home which most blacks just have to go on dreaming about decade after decade. It was in a first class suburban neighborhood just outside of San Francisco. My children were able to go to fine schools. There were lawns and trees and clean streets. For the first time in my life I was beginning to provide all the things a father normally wants for his children.

Marilyn had stuck with me through the long lean years. It was such a pleasure to reward her endurance with a measure of comfort and prosperity. What a thrill it was for her to be able to go into a supermarket and buy the things we really needed for a growing, active family. We had a new car for the first time, instead of models that had gathered troubles from each of the five preceding owners. I could plan my schedule for a whole month and not have to wonder if the car was going to be in the repair shop during any of the crucial moments.

In becoming a foreign missionary, I would have to give up all this financial security. Many people — especially my friends in black churches — felt that to go out with Overseas Crusades simply meant signing a contract that would cover my salary and all my expenses. Nothing would be farther from the truth. Every cent that I would spend for travel, for equipment, for moving the family to the Philippines, for my ministry expense as well as for my monthly allowance would have to be raised in gifts and monthly pledges. This, of course, is true for all missionaries going out with Overseas Crusades and not just for this black man.

I had left the Graham team by now, but invitations were still coming in faster than I could handle them. The Lord had provided so much for us and we gave continual thanks to Him.

But now was He saying to us: "I want you to give it all up and go to the foreign field"?

It was one thing for me to have the adventure of traveling through the Philippines, but now to pull up roots and take my family to live under the conditions that I had found there was something else.

Jumping ahead, I'll never forget Marilyn's reactions when we finally did get off the plane in Manila. Though I had tried to prepare the family for it, there was really no way to describe the heat and humidity. When we walked out of the air-conditioned plane and hit the thermal barrier outside, I wondered if the family would even make it into the airport, let alone make it for a whole year.

We reached the mission compound and moved into the World War II quonset hut which was to be our home.

It was almost like reliving those first years in the housing projects, except that these quonsets were made of G.I. sheeting instead of wood.

I must say, however, that the missionaries had really fixed up the quonsets nicely and we really enjoyed living in them. And so did the rats, mice, lizards and roaches, by the way. It was four or five months before Marilyn and some of the kids were able even to look at the lizards crawling across the walls without screaming.

We had lived with roaches before, of course, but these were something else. They were ugly monsters with armor plated bodies and creepy antennae. They died under the heavy blow of a shoe or paddle with a sickening crunch. The rats and mice were relatively bigger too. With the drainage ditches and open garbage containers as well as the raising of pigs and other livestock in the immediate area, it was impossible completely to control these pests.

The drinking water had to be boiled, flour had to be sifted to remove the uninvited guests, and nothing could be left out of the refrigerator without attracting an army of ants. They even had a breed of tiny red ants which could march around the ridges of a Mason jar with the lid screwed on tightly.

It was a new culture, and the kids had to get used to a new school — albeit a good missionary school. Keith was now 14, Carol 12, Adrienne 9 and David 6. There were so many adjustments for them to make.

As it turned out, Marilyn had to suffer and sacrifice the most. It was hard enough to adjust to these circumstances but doubly hard because my ministry kept me away from home more than three-fourths of the time. On top of this, Marilyn hardly had a single day free of tropical parasites in her intestines. "Manila Maneuvers" a missionary friend had called the malady.

As I have intimated, we learned to love the Philippines very much in spite of these circumstances, so much so that we stayed an extra year. It is a beautiful country, and the people really grow on you. As I write this book we are seriously considering another two-year stint in the Philippines.

The things that we thought would be hardships turned out not to be hardships at all. Furthermore, I gained a new appreciation for my own childhood experiences in the ghetto of San Francisco. Because of this background, I could much more readily identify with the problems and living conditions and frustrations of the Filipinos. I could talk intelligently about and be sensitive to their problems. It also gave me the opportunity to dispel their idea that all Americans are rich. As they understood more and more of my background, a strong bond developed which enhanced my ministry with them.

I could not foresee all this at the time, however, and these were some of the considerations that made that first decision extremely difficult.

There was still another factor. Why would the Lord be leading me away from America when I was just beginning to have a great ministry in dealing with the problems of our riot-torn country? It was such a crucial time on the racial scene. God had been using me to bring some understanding on both sides of the fence in certain areas. It seemed that conditions were getting worse and not better and so few were having any kind of voice that was heard.

"Are you really asking me to leave during this crucial time, Lord?" I had asked before coming to the Philippines.

My white friends were saying, "Bob, are you just becoming a coward and running away from the problem by going to the mission field? We need you here." Black friends were asking, "Bob, you are such an encouragement to many of us. How could the Lord be telling you to leave now?"

But Marilyn and I had that ingrained habit of trusting in the Lord with all our hearts, knowing that He would lead us in the paths we should go.

While we were still praying and seeking God's will in this matter, I had an interlude in Berlin as I attended the World Congress on Evangelism in October, 1966. There was only one chance in a thousand that it would happen, but the Lord arranged for the cards to be drawn so that Basil Costerisan and I were to room together. Basil was O.C.'s director in the Philippines and it was he who had made the request that we move there. Now the Lord had brought us together and Basil wasted no time before turning the screws.

One day during the Congress, Dick Hillis invited me to his room for further prayer about the Philippines. Dr. Ray Benson of the O.C. board who was traveling with Hillis was there along with Basil. Dr. Benson led in prayer. The words of his prayer were so moving that the Lord seemed to speak directly to my heart for the first time concerning the Philippines. He prayed with such assurance that when we finished the time of prayer, all of us were convinced beyond a shadow of a doubt that it was God's will for me to cancel our schedule in South America and accept the invitation to bring my family to the Philippines.

The conviction was so strong that immediately after prayer I said, "Dick, I'll go."

Then Dr. Benson said, "Bob, I believe this is of God and I think that you should call your wife and tell her immediately. Don't worry about the phone bill. I'll take care of that."

So I called Marilyn in South San Francisco and told her about our time of prayer and that I had decided that we should go to the Philippines as a family.

"Well, Bob, I already knew that, so your call comes as no surprise," Marilyn said. "I've been praying, too, and God has let me know that this is His will for our lives."

So now we had become one of the first black families to go out with an evangelical mission as foreign missionaries. Another wall had come tumbling down. God had broken out of the ghetto.

Again, true to His Word, God added all those other things. When we did come back from the Philippines after two years, He again opened tremendous doors of ministry, both in the U.S. and in a beautiful month-long trip in South America in March of 1970.

CHAPTER SEVENTEEN

It's a Brown World After All

Those wonderful Filipino people who instantly became our life-time friends provided some real insight into why my ministry was so well accepted all over Asia.

"We've heard so much about the black problem in America," a young Filipino said to me one day. "But you're not black, you're brown." He put his arm up to mine and sure enough, his skin was about the same shade as mine.

My dark skin, so long a problem to me and an impenetrable barrier for millions over the centuries, had become an advantage.

This incident was repeated dozens of times in the cities of Japan, Formosa, the Philippines, India, Indonesia, Singapore and Malaysia. It began to dawn on me that two-thirds of the world's population lives in Asia and the islands of the Pacific where skin colors vary in shades of brown. Add to this 325 million blacks in Africa and the dark skins of much of Latin America

119

and one must come to the conclusion that it's not only a small world but a brown world after all.

But skin color was just the beginning. I soon found an identification on a real gut level. Many of these brown and black peoples of the world have been exploited and subjugated by the white Westerners for centuries. They could easily identify with the problems that discrimination brought to the American black.

On one occasion, for instance, I appeared on one of the top T.V. shows in Manila. It started out as a routine interview with an American celebrity. I was introduced as a recording artist and they held up the jacket of my latest L.P. to the camera.

After I sang, the lady emcee asked how I could sing with such a sense of joy in my music. When I told her it was because of a profound religious experience and faith, she almost forgot that we were on the air until she had dug every detail of my conversion experience out of me.

When we finished she said, "You know, I have enjoyed talking with you so much. Somehow I don't look on you as an American or a foreigner. Our color is about the same, but more than that I just feel extremely comfortable talking with you. You seem just like one of us."

The more I lived with and ate with and ministered to Filipinos, the more I realized just how true this was. The American Negro and the Filipino are alike in their love for music. Everywhere one travels in the Orient, he finds that the hotel and restaurant combos are made up almost exclusively of Filipinos.

Our mannerisms, our behavior patterns, even our sense of time is similar. A running joke between American missionaries and their Filipino co-laborers is that of time. When a meeting is set, they always have to settle on whether they mean American time or Filipino time. If it's the former, you're speaking of a literal minute on the clock. If the latter, you're talking in a very general sense about a period of time that might end up being thirty minutes or an hour later.

Marilyn and I laughed the first time we heard this, as it reminded us instantly of what we call C.P. time — that is, colored people's time. We blacks are quite familiar with meetings, parties, and appointments that begin long past the agreed-upon time.

Filipinos as a whole, I found, enjoy a more easy-going life uncomplicated by a lot of things and activities. We match there also. We also have the common heritage of centuries of subjugation to the white man. In the Filipino's case, it was 333 years of Spanish rule and over 40 years of American control. In our case, it was generations of slavery and centuries of discrimination and segregation.

Dick Hillis had foreseen much of this potential rapport with Filipinos. At the same time, he had doubted that my ministry with the more truly Oriental and conservative Chinese would be as enthusiastically received as it turned out to be. But the crowds which jammed the crusades in Taiwan and Singapore proved again and again that my black heritage was a real passport.

My first trip with Norm Nelson into Asia was a winner and proved to me the way was open.

That I was the first Negro to minister in such a public way in Asia was one thing, and I'm sure there was a lot of curiosity connected with me. That Norm and I were traveling together brought a lot of attention as well. That winter of 1965 was just after the chaotic racial riots which saw so many of the inner cities burned. The Asian papers had been full of these reports and the people must have felt there was no contact between blacks and whites at all.

When Norm and I stepped off the planes in various cities together and then ministered together on the platform, people were amazed. If our audiences thought there was any strain between Norm and me, we quickly dispelled it.

At Soochow University in Taipei, for instance, Norm introduced me as being a black Swede. "All Swedish names end in 'son,'" he said. "My name is Nelson and I am a Swede. Bob's name is Harrison so he must be a Swede too."

I wasn't going to let him get away with that so I bounced up to the mike and used my old standby line: "Norm is trying to make me out to be something I'm not. But I want you to know that I really believe in integration. That's why I play both on the white keys and on the black keys of the piano."

This university crowd loved it. Our joking together about the race problem made them see there was really good harmony and love between us. The more I travel, the more I find there are racial problems everywhere. By our laughing and ministering together, Norm and I were able to demonstrate that Jesus is the answer to this worldwide problem.

This kind of impromptu humor went over so well that we began to increase our friendly insults. Sometimes I would introduce Norm as being a Negro who had a whitewash job, or I would say he was a Negro and I had frightened him so badly he turned white overnight. He got back at me by saying I had the biggest mouth of anyone he had ever known.

Working with Norm really did give me a tremendous introduction to the Orient. His powerful and beautiful tenor voice accompanied by full orchestra background on tape, our black and white banter and kidding on the platform, the fact that he was already so well-known in the Orient and especially the Philippines, all these were a tremendous help in introducing me to the Orient.

When I came back to the Philippines with my family, of course, I was now on my own. Would I make it?

Actually, having my family in the Philippines gave us even greater confirmation of the benefit of being black. Being a singer and a former evangelist with Billy Graham were a couple of things in my favor to start out with. Perhaps that had nothing to do with being black. But my family were just people. If they got on well with Filipinos it would have to be on their own.

Again that deep level of identification displayed itself. Almost from the first week we found a steady stream of Filipino wives and office girls with Philippine Crusades (the name used for Overseas Crusades in the Philippines) heading for our house to talk with Marilyn. We learned from the white missionaries that Marilyn had gained a much greater rapport and confidence with the Filipino girls in a few weeks than others had in several years. The Filipinos were always polite and friendly with the white American missionaries, but with Marilyn they immediately felt free to share their deepest thoughts and feelings. Marilyn's ministry in this way removed any final doubt in my mind that my ministry was so effective just because of the curiosity in Filipinos seeing a black man or the entertainment value of my singing.

We had planned to be in the Philippines for only a year, but we ended up jamming two fantastic years full of ministries in Okinawa, Taiwan, Singapore, Malaysia, Indonesia and Ceylon as well as a dozen cities in the Philippines. During this period I even participated in a crusade in the Democratic Republic of Congo where we saw over 7,000 of the 87,000 attending come forward in the final meeting.

I had meetings under almost every conceivable circumstance and in every kind of place. I was in homes, mayors' and governors' offices, high schools, colleges, universities, Lion's Clubs, Rotary Clubs, radio stations, television stations, prayer breakfast sessions, Sunday school conventions, pastor's conferences, army camps and hospitals, servicemen's centers, business luncheon meetings, Bible schools, evangelism seminars, churches, city-wide crusades, rallies, street meetings and press conferences.

These appearances and crusades in the Philippines and the rest of the countries to which I traveled were always marked by hundreds of people coming to know the Lord -- undoubtedly at least as many as if I were white. And there was constant evidence that my blackness was actually contributing to the success of meetings and crusades. Day after day and month after month I was proving to myself that the black Christian was wanted — even desperately needed. And day after day, month after month, I was praying and longing for the time when hosts of my black brothers in Christ would discover this fact and act upon it. Would the day ever come?

Of necessity, my crusades outside the Philippines were characterized by my appearing just in time to preach and sing the first night and by my leaving after the last Asian had come to the altar to begin a new life in Christ. I was warmly accepted in these cases as a platform personality, but what would happen were it required of me to struggle through all the nitty-gritty of the organizational preparation of the crusade? Could I work shoulder to shoulder as a bona fide team member with Asians?

The answer to this came in our first major city-wide crusade in the Philippines. After various warm-up crusades in scattered cities of the Philippines with its 7,107 islands, we were invited to Bacolod City, the sugar capital of the country.

Realizing we needed more thorough preparation and teamwork in this crusade, we sent down one of the young Philippine Crusade staff members several weeks in advance. His name was Jun (for junior) Galope, and he turned out to be the key to a greatly expanded ministry. Jun and I became an inseparable team for the remainder of the two years and this brown Filipino-black American combination became a thing of beauty.

The invitation for the crusade had originally come from only one of the nine relatively small evangelical churches in this city of some 200,000 people. Jun's first accomplishment was to get five other churches cooperating in spite of the fact that they had had some differences over the years.

From these six churches he organized eighty weekly prayer cells. He helped the churches raise a budget of over $2,000.00, a princely sum in this nation where the annual per capita income is less than $100.00. From among the local people he organized committees for promotion, finance, program, follow-up and other activities, such as construction of a platform large enough to hold the 200-voice choir that he had encouraged into being.

Jun helped the local people get one hour of free television time as well as dozens of hours of radio time. This later included a daily rebroadcast of the previous night's meeting on the local commercial stations. Posters and streamers were all over the city. When I arrived in town, I was motorcaded from the airport and around the center of town. It was probably as well organized a crusade as any ever held in the Philippines up to that time, comparing favorably with the Billy Graham crusades held in the Philippines in 1963. It was a remarkable accomplishment for this 27-year-old Filipino in his native land whose population is 85 percent Roman Catholic.

The crusade began on a Sunday night as several hundred formed a torchlight procession. Such torch processions are a familiar sight in the Catholic Philippines, but this was the first time the Protestants of Bacolod had ever shown their strength. They streamed to the crusade site from four directions, coordinated by a radio broadcast and scores of transistor radios carried by the marchers. The mayor of the city joined the procession to open the crusade officially. As the torches passed the huge Roman Catholic Church on the plaza, droves of worshipers streaming out of the Palm Sunday mass joined the procession and followed it to the crusade meeting.

Billboards all over town for days had been proclaiming that something wonderful was coming to the Seawall, the public meeting place on the shores of the bay. After the crusade began, these signs were changed to read "Something Wonderful Is Happening at the Seawall." The slogan caught on, and reports came from many that people in the shops all over town could be heard talking about the wonderful happenings at the Seawall.

The huge crowd which occupied every seat the first night was attributed to the fact that it was Palm Sunday. But fears that Monday would bring a drop proved groundless when every seat was again filled, including 2,000 extra chairs put up. Each night the seating capacity was enlarged — ultimately by constructing crude lumber benches. And each night every seat was filled with hundreds more standing. The crowds grew until the final night when a careful count revealed that 10,000 were there.

The response to the invitations grew apace. On the Friday youth night more than 250 came forward and a similar number responded on the final night. In the eight-day crusade 1,252 came forward to put their trust in the Savior. Each of these was counseled personally by church members whom Jun had trained. In the following weeks local church attendance swelled as many of these converts submitted to baptism and church membership.

This very successful crusade was followed by several others in the months that followed. Then just before I was to return to the States with my family after the two-year hitch, Jun took on the almost impossible task of organizing and coordinating not one but *five* back-to-back city-wide crusades. These were held in eastern Mindanao, the huge island that makes up the southernmost part of the Philippines. In Davao, the major city in the area, fifteen evangelical churches made an unforgettable impact on their community in a way similar to Bacolod. This eight-day crusade was followed immediately with five-day crusades in four smaller towns within a radius of forty miles of Davao. More than 2,000 people ultimately came to know the Lord through these meetings.

The teamwork and unity of spirit required for a really successful crusade is perhaps not fully appreciated by anyone who has never been involved. Evangelists and their co-workers are really quite human, and the number of things that can go wrong in a big crusade can strain relationships to the breaking point, even with those of the same cultural background. But the FilAm team of Jun and myself and many others involved was priceless.

There have been many times since those days in the Philippines when I would have given my right arm to have Jun setting up my crusades. He has an ability and drive and zeal and spiritual depth and understanding that I have seen matched only on rare occasions.

Our two years as foreign missionaries in the Philippines all too soon came to a close. There were sad and tearful good-byes to our Filipino friends as we boarded the ship to return home. Part of our hearts will always remain in Asia and we are still hoping that the Lord will take us back someday.

We will bring one fitting "souvenir" back with us. Little Steven was born just a few months after our return to the States. We understand that the staff of Philippine Crusades got quite a kick out of the picture with the caption: "Steven Harrison. Made in the Philippines."

What a thrill it would be if someday Steven returned to his point of origin as a soldier of the cross. By then, dear God, may there be a host of black missionaries there to greet him.

CHAPTER EIGHTEEN

The Devil Didn't Like It

I suppose that one test of a good idea is to see how strongly an enemy fights against it. I took no comfort from this thought during one particular bout with the devil, but his interest in destroying a plan of mine gives reassurance as I look back.

The idea came to me after we had completed our first year as a family in the Philippines. After the crusade in Kinshasa, Congo, I flew to the States where I had various obligations to fulfill. As I traveled from city to city, the Lord wouldn't stop bothering me with the concern of getting black Christians to the mission fields of the world.

I didn't need to be reminded of the shallow concept most black churches have of missions. A typical "missionary" service consists of women dressing up in white and attending a meeting where they take up an offering to help some family pay a bill or buy food. If one would come in and mention William Carey or Hudson Taylor they wouldn't know whom you were talking about. There would be few men at the meeting and no young people.

There wouldn't be any foreign missionary volunteers coming out of those meetings, I knew.

Christian camping centers, missionary conferences, evangelical schools, all these, I believed, would some-day provide an answer. But what about all the capable young blacks who were academically and spiritually qualified right now? What about the great opportunities around the world that couldn't wait? Would we have to wait years for a trickle of blacks to come in contact with white missionary work, to be accepted by and trained in white schools, and to be sent out by white organizations?

I was wrestling with the Lord in prayer when a thought struck me. I had been challenged for missions by seeing them in action around the world. Why not organize a tour of leading black ministers and let them see the opportunities firsthand? Wouldn't they return to their pulpits and preach foreign missions?

It was a wild idea. Who would go? Where would the money come from? How could I organize such a tour since I was due to go back to Manila in less than a week? I had a tiger by the tail. I was scared of the idea, but I couldn't let it go, either.

Feeling a little foolish, I flew down to L.A. to see my good friends Rev. Earl Pleasant, pastor of Mt. Moriah Baptist Church, and Rev. E. V. Hill, pastor of Zion Baptist Church. Both of these churches are large and influential in the black community and are two of the few who have any significant foreign missionary program.

I talked with Earl first, but didn't have the nerve to tell him what I had in mind. "What in the world can we do to get our people involved in foreign missions?" I asked Earl. "I know your church is involved, and Ed

Hill's is, but how can we get the rest of the black constituency conscious of the needs and opportunities in foreign missions?"

"Well, Bob," he said, "you've traveled quite a bit and are knowledgeable about mission activity. Why don't you formulate a minister's tour to a mission field? Take them out there and let them be exposed to missions and also get them involved in a ministry."

I didn't question anymore whether this was God's will!

We talked with Ed Hill who quickly became enthused with the idea. Both men promised to go and bring others with them. We felt that twenty-five ministers would be a manageable group and also large enough to make an impact on the black church. I didn't know where they would come from or how I would go about taking them on a tour of the Orient, but I whispered a prayer and plunged ahead.

By now, I had only a couple of days left before returning to the Philippines, but I wrote letters to pastors in Southern California and Texas, contacting a Christian travel agent who promised to help all he could, and then turned the coordinating work over to my secretary in San Francisco as I flew off for the Philippines.

Letters soon began pouring into my box in Manila and we quickly filled up our quota of twenty-five.

The real development and coordination of the tour began. I was in constant comunication with the travel agent, my secretary in San Francisco, the ministers in California and Texas and I was also doing a lot of leg work overseas. I made a special trip to Taiwan to set up the arrangements for our tour there. In the Philippines I was working very hard with our new Field Director, Jim Montgomery, co-author of this book.

The tour looked like a real winner. The ministers would experience missionary work in the large cities and in the small barrios and towns and everything in between. Certainly it would quicken their interest in sending out missionaries to the fields of the world.

Then the roof began to cave in.

First of all, two ministers became critically ill and had to cancel out. Then smouldering racial tensions burst into flame in several parts of the country, forcing two more leading pastors and several of their friends to cancel out. Even the weather worked against us. Heavy rains in Southern California caused extensive destruction of property to several of the members of Ed Hill's church and he felt he must stay and help them. A death in Earl Pleasant's church ruled him out. With Ed and Earl, my close friends on whom I had counted most, went several whom they had invited to go with them.

The enemy had pulled out his big guns: illness, riots, floods and death. We were down to six. Should I forget it?

On top of this, my own body was screaming for mercy. I had abused it just too much. I went to a leading physician in Manila. He told me that if my body hadn't been very strong in the first place, it long since would have collapsed. He warned me that I needed several weeks of complete rest or else I faced a physical breakdown.

I had a long talk with Jim Montgomery and we had prayer together. "Could it possibly be that God is saying that we should cancel the tour until the following year?" Jim asked.

When he lined up the great number of cancellations with my weakened physical condition, plus the fact that I would have five demanding city-wide crusades coming up immediately after the ministers' tour, he counseled that perhaps this was the Lord's way of saying that it was a good idea but not the right time.

He pointed out that by postponing the tour a year we could get the key ministers who had canceled out and also that it would be much easier to coordinate a tour when I was back in the States. I told Jim that I had been thinking along the same lines, but that I thought we ought to pray a little more about it.

About two weeks later I received four letters almost simultaneously from key ministers assuring me that they would be part of the tour. Two of them said they were bringing one other minister with them. They had already taken their shots, they had paid part of their tickets, and they were looking forward to the time with great anticipation.

Against Jim's good advice and all common sense, I knew I couldn't let these six ministers down. The possibility of creating a whole new dimension in the ministry of the Negro Church had gripped me too hard.

I had a new problem now. As tour director for twenty-five ministers, I could receive a free round trip ticket to San Francisco to meet them and bring them back. With six, I was just another paying customer. I was physically worn, mentally spent and spiritually almost incapacitated. The bank balance was low, but I scraped all the way to the bottom of it and flew to San Francisco.

Even then Satan didn't let up. In San Francisco I received a long distance call from Dr. Robert Wilson of Dallas, Texas. He said that he had been on the way to the plane when a death took place in his family. He was paged at the airport and returned home. His companion canceled out with him.

We had been through a slugging match with the devil, and I'll have to admit that he all but had us whipped. A few more good solid blows and it could have been all over.

He did keep swinging, but his jabs at this point were

those of a beaten man on the way down. When the five of us met in San Francisco, for instance, I found that two of the ministers somehow didn't have visas for the Philippines. We had just one day to get them, which seemed an absolute impossibility. The Lord pulled this one off, however, and we left for Tokyo on the first leg of the tour.

There was one last desperate lunge. In route, the pilot was notified that the worst snow storm in 100 years was sealing off Tokyo and that we wouldn't be able to land there. We watched drearily and not without some concern as the pilot dumped thousands of pounds of fuel into the ocean and then made a landing at Wake Island.

Later that day we took off again, but were diverted to Osaka, Japan, where we spent a night and a day. The plans for ministry in Tokyo were canceled. The next day, March 12, we took off for Taiwan and it was as if God said, "Okay, devil, you've had your licks. From now on I'm taking over."

And He did.

CHAPTER NINETEEN

Gideon's Army

Gideon's mighty army of twenty-five black ministers was down to a mere four. I've given the devil a lot of credit for whittling down our number, and there is no doubt in my mind that he was after our hides.

But I'm also convinced that God wasn't going to let him have the victory. The Lord let him have a go at us, but at the same time He was testing our faith and cutting the number down of those He wanted on the tour. The comparison with Gideon is not inappropriate, I feel. The four pastors represented a good cross section of a vast majority of the black church in America, and two of them held top positions in their denominations. Dr. E. Stanley Branch pastors a church of 4,000 members in Houston, Texas, and is also a leader in the five-million member National Baptist Convention. Dr. Floyd Williams, also a pastor in Houston, is secretary-treasurer of the missions department of the Progressive Baptist Convention with two million members. The Reverends Ralph Houston and C. D. Toliver were pastors from Los Angeles representing the United Holy Church of

America and the African Methodist Episcopal Church respectively. These are two more of the influential denominations of the black church.

Besides having these leading men on the tour, we were also making a 16 mm color film which ultimately would be shown in hundreds of black churches. This in itself, I felt, made up for the ministers who canceled out.

Two hours after we landed in Taipei, Taiwan, we were hustled into a T.V. studio for the first of many, many appearances during a seven-day stay. The next day each of us was assigned either to a Chinese or American missionary and we headed for five different parts of the island.

What stories these men had to tell when we assembled back in Taipei five days later. Floyd Williams, for instance, was taken to Tungshih in central Taiwan where Norwegian missionary Johan Johansen had set up a meeting for him with a group of students.

"Right away they expected me to sing," he told us in exaggerated astonishment. "Man, you know I can't carry a tune in a bucket."

We all heartily agreed to that. "But they wouldn't take no for an answer," he went on. "They must have thought that all Negroes were singers. They begged and they pleaded and finally pushed me up in front of the crowd. I was really on the spot so I unloaded 'Down by the Riverside.' Man, it was the sorriest mess you ever heard. But what could I do?" We doubled up in laughter.

Floyd also preached in meetings Friday and Saturday night and all day Sunday. No one, however, repeated the request for a special number.

C. D. Toliver and Stanley Branch were taken to the southern tip of Taiwan where Finnish Lutheran missionaries carried on medical, radio and evangelistic ministries. They ministered in various places including one building that had no roof. In a touching moment C. D. Toliver shared his faith in Jesus Christ with patients in a polio hospital. Toliver had fallen victim to polio in his youth, and this made his testimony especially meaningful. They were particularly interested in the specially made shoe that he wore, for many of the patients were crippled in a similar way.

Six-foot-four, 278-pound Ralph Houston was quite naturally the center of attention wherever he went. "There I was walking down the street with a white missionary (Les Wait of O.C.) and a couple of Chinese Christians," he told us. "Because of my huge body and black skin I attracted mobs of children and adults. Here was this huge crowd of people following us down the street, all chattering in Chinese. Even Les Wait was using the dialect. Suddenly it dawned on me that I was the only one of my color and my kind. It made me a bit nervous. For the first time I really felt what it means to be a foreigner."

Ralph went to Peikang, the religious and superstitious capital of Taiwan. Thousands of Chinese make the pilgrimage yearly to Peikang to worship the goddess Matsu. It is said that nearly half of the people of the city make their living from some type of income derived from the temple and its activities. Some liken it to the Biblical city of Ephesus and its goddess Diana. Peikang has consistently resisted the Gospel and clung to its superstitions. The Presbyterians, Baptists and Lutherans have small churches there, but they have grown slowly.

Ralph Houston with his bulk and black skin attracted probably the biggest crowd the Baptist church had ever had. He told them that he had come not to talk about a Negro god or an American god or even a Taiwanese god but about the God who had created us all and loves us all very much. Helen Berry, the Baptist missionary there, said that the nine who came forward at the invitation represented the biggest evangelistic response in the history of the church.

I spent the weekend in Pingtung where the Covenant church was in the midst of an evangelistic campaign. A good number came to know the Lord in the three nights I preached.

Since we were scattered to the smaller towns of Taiwan, we gained genuine Oriental experiences that we would have missed had we stayed only in the capital. The ministers learned not only how to get the strange Chinese foods to their mouths with chopsticks, but also how to swallow it in spite of the sometimes unsanitary conditions. They showed their best manners to the great pleasure of these humble Chinese folk, and no one picked up a stomach problem along the way.

There was an overwhelming acceptance and response from the Chinese as well as American missionaries with many requests to return.

Hong Kong, our next stop, provided an entirely different type of experience. We checked into the Hong Kong Hilton and for a day we hit the normal shopping centers where the average tourist goes. We therefore saw the glittering face of Hong Kong first.

On the second day, we stepped into a different world, one these ministers hardly knew existed. By this time I had been to Hong Kong several times, but this was the first experience for these men.

An FEBC missionary, the Rev. Bob Larson, and a Chinese national took us into the walled city of Kowloon. This is a city in itself and is controlled by the communists. Its filth, its depravity, its inhuman living conditions are almost indescribable. Inside the walls the tin-roofed houses are jam-packed together. These houses at most have one or two rooms with as many as sixteen living in one room.

The tiny "streets" are barely wide enough for single file pedestrian traffic in each direction. They are filled with garbage and debris. The stench is overwhelming.

With these, of course, come rats, filth and disease.

In this miserable city, crime, vice, and dope run rampant.

On this same day we saw other parts of refugee-choked Hong Kong. We saw children sleeping on the sidewalks where refugee families try to eke out a meager income by selling trinkets on the streets.

We saw the huge, high-rise apartment buildings where thousands of Chinese are packed into one tiny area. We saw the boat people — hundreds and hundreds of them — living, marrying, giving birth and dying while afloat in the waters of Hong Kong harbor.

Amid these terrible living conditions we saw the white American missionaries struggling to reach these people with the Gospel. A most beautiful sight is to see several hundred children on their way to the roof-top schools. Without these missionary schools on the roof tops of dozens of buildings, thousands of Chinese would grow up with no education and little hope of improving their lot in life. And thousands, of course, would grow up without ever hearing the name of Jesus.

We saw missionaries running orphanages and churches and doing almost everything humanly possible to alleviate the misery and being a spiritual hope to these forlorn people.

It was a different group of black pastors who returned to their plush Hilton Hotel that night. They had seen human beings living in conditions worse than even their dogs at home would have experienced. They had seen thousands upon thousands of squatters claiming a tiny piece of land and building "homes" out of whatever scraps of wood and tin and cardboard they could beg, borrow, or literally steal. They had known poverty and depravation and discrimination in America, but this was something else. As we returned to our hotel room, I could almost sense a feeling of shame that we could walk into such comfortable surroundings, knowing the conditions under which people just down the street were living.

"We've got to come back and bring many more ministers," said one of the fellows. "We've got to bring some laymen, too. So many of our people are so preoccupied in their little world in the U.S. that they're always full of complaints. If we can just bring some more folks over here, they will become sensitive to what Christ meant when He said, 'Go ye into all the world and preach the Gospel to every creature.'"

Each stop on the tour, I believe, gave us a different dominant impression. In Taiwan we ministered. In Hong Kong, this great materialistic tourist Mecca, we paradoxically were impressed most of all with the physical needs of man. In the Philippines, we were overwhelmed by the eagerness with which we were received as blacks.

We landed in Manila at three in the afternoon and without leaving the airport immediately flew to Bacolod, that city which had been so turned on by our crusades at the Seawall. A reception committee of about sixty-five met us at the airport. There was a huge banner, and as we entered the terminal two or three *sampaguita* leis were draped over our shoulders by a group of lovely university girls.

We were introduced to the leading clergymen and civic leaders and then motorcaded into and through the heart of Bacolod City. Cars aren't readily available in the Philippines, but they had about twenty-five jeepneys and automobiles of various descriptions following a police escort with sirens howling.

That evening we were entertained at a banquet of

about 100 church and city leaders. The mayor officially welcomed us and the governor of the province sent his greetings. He had planned to attend, but was called away to Manila for a conference with President Marcos.

Each of us was asked to say a few words. Floyd Williams was first. He stood up and told some very sad jokes but the people were polite enough to laugh. They just seemed so glad to have us there that anything was warmly accepted.

The mayor made much of the fact that we were the first delegation of Negroes ever to come to Bacolod. "I'm doubly glad that this delegation happens to be a group of Negro clergymen," he said.

It was quite late before the banquet broke up, but we were aroused for a 6:00 a.m. breakfast and tour of the city beginning at 7:30. We were given the choice of a motor tour of the city or one on foot. Our hosts were pleased that the black ministers wanted to walk so that they could get closer to the people.

Five black Americans attracted a lot of attention. Many of the people had never seen blacks before, especially if they were too young to remember the American G.I. during World War II or had not been to one of my crusades there.

Many of the children would run up and touch us and keep saying, "black Americano, black Americano."

"Huh, just think of this," big Ralph Houston said expansively, "a black man walking the street like a celebrity and being touched by everyone."

Our ministers felt even more like celebrities that afternoon when a press conference was called for our benefit.

But that night topped all. The city sponsored a panel discussion in the 7,000-seat auditorium of West Negros College, the largest hall in the city. Ralph Toliver, an accomplished classical singer, and I entertained and then we sat down with the panel. Included in the group were publishers of two local newspapers, a high school principal, a university professor and a sociologist. The meeting was covered by radio and T.V. and the auditorium was crowded to capacity.

Our black ministers were overwhelmed. They might have expected a warm welcome from a handful of Christians, but here was a whole city embracing them.

The forum discussion itself revolved around the racial problem in America. We were forthright in our answers and even alluded to the racial problems all over the world, including the Philippines. I had observed that dark-skinned Filipinos are sometimes the recipients of discrimination in some forms. And of course the racial tensions between the Filipinos and Chinese, and Filipinos and Moslems are a great source of irritation in the Philippines. Some were shocked that we would bring such things out in the open, but by and large they appreciated our candidness.

After the more formal discussion from the platform, the session was thrown open for questions from the floor. Someone wanted to know why we had not come before. "We were told that we weren't wanted," said one of our blacks.

But the rejoinders came back: "Oh, yes we do. We do want you. Your coming has already made a contribution. You have helped us understand the racial problem and we feel you understand us."

Then someone stood up — it must have been a Christian — and asked point blank if we were planning to send a black missionary back to stay. We said this was definitely what we wanted to do but the young man wasn't satisfied. "Are you really going to send someone or are you just being polite?"

My minister friends said not only that they were coming back but that they wanted to bring others with them. As God would have it, at that very moment Jim Montgomery had on his desk in Manila a letter requesting that we sponsor a black graduate student from Wheaton College for the summer. Within a few weeks, then, we had a black short-term missionary living in Bacolod. Where the full-time missionary is going to come from, I don't know. Perhaps someone reading these words will be the one.

After Bacolod, our group headed for Cebu City and then Davao where Jun Galope was in the last days of pre-crusade activity. The ministers were able to get in on some of this, but had to leave before the crusade actually began.

Before leaving, Dr. Branch summed up what all the men had been saying: "The time is ripe. I feel black missionaries must go to every nation. This has been one of the richest experiences of my life."

The completion of the tour of black ministers marked the beginning of the writing of this book. As a result, I can't at this time give a glowing account of any transformed churches or of a host of blacks who began setting their sights on the foreign field after these ministers returned to their churches and denominations. Even if I could, I'm sure it would only be a small part of what still needs to be done.

I am sure, however, that it was a significant beginning. If a host of such tours were made, there is no doubt in my mind but that it would begin the transformation of the black Church so desperately needed in America.

CHAPTER TWENTY

But What Can I Do?

If you are white and a Christian and have read this far, I believe chances are pretty good that you really want to do something about the black potential for God in our midst.

Though there are plenty of racists in our churches, I believe there must be a great silent majority of people like yourself who honestly don't know what they can do. They are silent primarily because they are removed from the problem. They are not excluding blacks — they just don't know any blacks. They aren't the ones keeping blacks out of churches and conference grounds and seminaries and missionary conferences. Wrapped up in their own problems and their own enthusiasms, they simply are unaware of that great black exclusion.

This could not have been brought more forcefully home to me than at the World Congress on Evangelism in Berlin in 1966. Here was the leading evangelistic organization of our century calling the peoples of the world together to consider the lofty subject of "One Task, One Gospel, One Race."

There was much elaboration on this theme with position papers, lectures, and discussion groups. But the emphasis was almost exclusively on "one task" and "one Gospel." There was no position paper on "one race."

Ostensibly we were there to discuss for at least one third of the time "one race." We were from all the races of the world, and the matter of race was one of the crucial problems of that world. Yet the whole subject was virtually ignored. There were many at the Congress, myself included, who believed that one of the greatest hindrances to the Gospel was the fact that we Christians didn't consider ourselves one race. We considered ourselves to be many different races and we tended to isolate ourselves along racial and national lines.

As the Congress was drawing to an end and we began to realize how lightly the subject was being treated, a number of Negro delegates got together and confronted Dr. Carl Henry with this omission.

I should say it was not just American blacks who were disturbed with the problem. Delegations from such places as India, South America, Africa and the Orient also felt the omission. As I have brought out elsewhere in this book, there is a growing revulsion among the emerging peoples of the world to the idea that the white races are superior.

This certainly is a vivid illustration on the grand scale of what I have been talking about. The problem of the black Christian is so far removed from the white evangelical that even when he gets together for a World Congress to talk about one race, he inadvertently overlooks the whole issue.

The beauty of the whole situation, however, is that once confronted with it the Congress was quick to make a change. It was too late to include any position papers or discussion groups, but the Congress was preparing a final statement relating to its theme.

When we confronted Dr. Carl Henry with the omission, he immediately apologized for the omission and put us to work developing a statement about "one race" to be included in this final paper.

A number of us worked into the late hours. Some of those present besides myself were Jimmy McDonald, Dr. Howard Jones, Ralph Bell, the Rev. Lewis Johnson, and the Rev. James E. Massey of the Church of God.

Our statement spoke to some of the injustices and sins of the evangelicals in their exclusion of minority groups. It addressed some of the issues relating to race and evangelism.

This part of the final statement really put a spotlight on the problem. I believe this was a tremendous victory. The results of the Congress were publicized around the world. The inclusion of such a strong statement about "one race" in the final paper has done much already to get people stirred up about what they can do. Some things have already been accomplished.

I take a great deal of encouragement from this. A great host of white Christians are ready to become involved, I believe, if they are just made aware of the problem and shown in a practical way what they can do.

Where can you start? Well, by reading this book you have already begun. Perhaps our biggest problem is one of an information gap between the white and black evangelical. By graciously taking time out to read my story, you have become much more aware of the real situation and the things that separate the two races. Perhaps for the first time you have become aware of the black brother as being a real identity.

There are many other good books on the market, both evangelical* and secular. These can further enlighten you. You should subscribe to *Ebony* Magazine, a black publication which can be picked up at almost any news stand. You'll find it to be a quality, entertaining and

* Tom Skinner's *Black and Free* and *Words of Revolution,* both published by Zondervan, are excellent and informative.

realistic periodical. It will keep you up to date with good articles and will review the books that will be most enlightening and helpful. Then share this information and literature with others. Get your friends to read the books and articles that shed light on the subject. Include in your discussion and training classes at church the place of the black Christian in world evangelism today. Get your pastor to speak on the subject. There is no substitute for this first step of a wide scattering of information.

Secondly, there is no escaping the Biblical pattern of righting a wrong by confession of sin. In many cases it might be primarily sins of omission and apathy rather than outright prejudice and racism. It should be personal confession as well as corporate confession by the local church, by denominations and by the Church as a whole in America. As you read on in this chapter perhaps more and more things will come to mind that need to be confessed.

Use a little imagination in your prayer and confession. The church has always been a minority and through the ages has been persecuted in one form or another. You should be able to identify with the black Christian who has carried the load of double minority persecution — being black and being an evangelical Christian.

Thirdly, I feel that the white Christian of America must once and for all flush from his mind those tricky theological rationalizations about the curse of the black man. The evangelical racist still uses the ninth chapter of Genesis to prove that the black man is cursed of God and therefore should be separate.

They preach that the curse of God was on all Hamites and that the Hamites were Negroes.

It's a ridiculous notion, of course, and would hardly deserve any attention except for the fact that some still preach it and many still have some residue of this idea in their minds.

If one takes a literal view of the passage he finds first of all that the curse was on Canaan, Ham's son, and not on Ham himself. Overlooking that, they then try to divide the peoples of the world into black, Oriental and white by saying that Ham was a Negro, Shem became the founder of the Oriental races, and Japheth the founder of the white races.

It's a wild theory at best and certainly not supported by careful scientific study let alone good Bible exegesis.

One shred of evidence that is referred to is that the Hebrew word for Ham means dark color or swarthy. This is interpreted to apply to Negroes.

But of course there are swarthy Greeks, Indians, Spaniards, Filipinos or any number of peoples around the world.

Even if it were true that the Negro race was cursed along with the curse of Ham, what do we do with the work of Jesus Christ on Calvary which obliterated all curses and all sins? The whole idea is just too much to swallow. I hope the thinking Christians of America will bury this wild hypothesis.

An even more absurd attempt to drag segregation out of the Bible comes from Paul's message at Athens recorded in Acts 17:26. It says, "And he made from one every nation of men to live on all the face of the earth, having determined alloted periods and the boundaries of their habitation."

Even if this verse did support segregation, how anyone could get out of this that just Negroes should be segregated is beyond me. If we're going to segregate on the basis of this verse, we're going to have to segregate our Swedes and our Italians and our Greeks and our Jews and our Orientals and everyone else in America.

Furthermore, let's stop calling the black Christian "our dear colored brother," as if he were a separate category of Christian. It's quite apparent what color I am. I can't hide that. I can even be kidded about it. But when I am categorized as being another kind of a Christian, then we are missing the great, beautiful thing that Jesus Christ brought: There is a oneness in Christ that overshadows all other differences.

After being informed and after confessing and cleansing our minds of all stupid racial prejudices, then the white Christian must in the fourth place, begin to *do* something. I have often found in talking with people that they imply that because they can't do everything, they can't do anything. What they really must mean is that they *don't want* to do anything. They don't want to become involved. Why go out of the way to look for trouble?

Jesus could have said that about all of the races. Why become involved in humanity? What would it bring him but sorrow and pain and grief?

There is no way we can serve the Lord effectively without becoming involved. And there is no way to help the Negro serve the Lord effectively without becoming involved.

The least you can do is to insist on a series of exchanges in your church. Think what it would do for the church of Jesus Christ all over America if the white churches invited black pastors and black singers and black converts to give their testimonies. The lines of communication would be opened. Understanding would begin. Even love would blossom as blacks and whites found the great unifying factor of love for Jesus Christ being a common bond that surmounts all other obstacles.

And by the way, don't *just* invite black musicians. That only perpetuates the stereotype that blacks are very musical. There is more to us than that.

Exchanges will help the black realize that he has something to give as well as something to get. But there are other activities typically held in white churches that the blacks need to experience. The next time your church holds a missionary or Bible conference you ought to invite delegations from black churches to attend and provide a bus to pick them up if necessary. Their experiences in these areas are so limited that they wouldn't know where to start on their own. But by observing and participating in what you are doing, they will quickly learn and will begin doing the same in their churches. It will be all the better if you have blacks participating on the platform in these conferences to help your guests identify with the program.

You will have some opposition to this in your church. But somewhere along the line someone must be willing to stand on conviction and do what is right and necessary. The time for mere talk has surely long since passed.

Another thing you can do is to begin putting pressure on Christian schools and seminaries, conference grounds and missionary organizations. If a host of white Christians began doing this, each in his own circle of influence, the tide would be irresistible.

You can take that step farther. Many such institutions are now eager to include blacks but don't know how to contact them or how to get them to attend. This was the question in a group of leaders with whom I was talking at Mt. Hermon. They wanted blacks at their conferences but the plaintive question always was, "How can we get them here?"

Whites must actively seek the participation of blacks. We blacks are so ignorant of what is commonly available to the white Christian that you are going to have to make an effort to inform us. Then you're going to have to make a determined effort to convince us we are really wanted.

Every black Christian in America has had dozens of experiences where he has been offered something but only in politeness. He must not only hear that he is welcome, but he must see demonstrated that he is definitely wanted.

In many cases this might even involve subsidizing blacks. The history of excluding blacks has been too long and too deep for you to simply sit back and say that any black can come who wants to. Think what it would mean if you as an individual or if your local church sponsored some black young people to a summer conference. It would undoubtedly make a great spiritual impact on their lives as well as help them and the white campers become acquainted in a natural setting. In knocking about the grounds for a week together, black and white kids would discover just what normal human beings the people of each group are.

If this were done on a wide scale throughout the country, we would soon see blacks pouring into our Christian schools, into pulpits around the country and into evangelistic and missionary organizations. The great black potential would begin to be developed for the cause of Christ.

Right now and certainly as more and more black Christian leaders are being trained, every evangelical organization should have a strong recruitment program to include Negroes. If each of these organizations used any part of the ingenuity they have put to work in getting the white Christian to part with his dollar in meeting this issue, we would see the black church coming to life.

Another thing. I have honestly written that the point of what I am saying is not to get churches integrated. This is a side issue. But it still is a tragic thing to see the white churches fleeing from the inner cities as black Christians move in. When the neighborhood starts turning black, the white Christian can't get out of there fast enough. Then, having abandoned his ministry, the white Christian wants to sell his church to the black Christians moving in. This only perpetuates the conditions excluding Negroes from the challenge and training and inspiration they would get in white evangelical circles.

Frequently, this means selling the church to a "liberal" black church. If you would ask the pastor if he believed in the virgin birth, or miracles, or the resurrection and so on, he would say that he did. But if you began asking members if they had ever personally committed their lives to Jesus Christ for salvation they would not understand. The Gospel as such has never been clearly presented to them. The only invitation they have ever heard from the pulpit is the pastor saying, "The doors of the church are now open." By this he means to say that everyone ought to be a church member and you are now invited to join.

"Give me your hand and God your heart," he says. Anyone coming forward to join the church either by "profession of faith" or baptism is immediately voted in by a motion from someone in the congregation and a raising of hands. I have never seen anyone turned down.

By "profession of faith" the new member means that he gives mental assent to the historical Jesus. He believes all that the Bible says. But it is an historical belief. The truths of the Bible are usually related to social justice and not spiritual life. He does not deny the cardinal doctrines but at the same time he does not know about a personal relationship with Jesus Christ.

When your church flees the approaching black tide and sells out to a black congregation, this is the spiritual ministry you are leaving behind. Aren't you proud of yourself?

How beautiful it would be if instead of this the white

churches of our cities would follow a suggestion I made to an Assemblies of God church in east Oakland. They left the black neighborhood as it enveloped them. Nothing wrong here. But instead of abandoning the church, my suggestion was that they sell it to the mission board of the denomination. They in turn could develop a black church with a black pastor who was strongly evangelical and would really meet the spiritual needs of the community. We can't begin to say we are going into all the world to preach the Gospel if we deny this wonderful message to the very ones moving into our neighborhoods.

Your church may not be in such an inner city community — most congregations have already fled to the suburbs (something that needs confessing?) — but you can still "mother" a church in ghetto areas. Again, the Assemblies denomination has begun to really think about this. In a top level meeting gathered specifically to talk about the black church problem, it was suggested that if every district of the denomination provided buildings and black pastors for one ghetto church, the denomination would immediately have forty-seven new congregations. It is such creative thinking that is going to make a difference in the problem we face.

There is just no end to the amount of things you and your church can do if you'll just apply some ingenuity and brainstorming creativity to the problem. All the bases, from ghetto Sunday schools and vacation Bible schools to helping sponsor black pastors to missionary tours, can be touched.

Somewhere along the line someone is going to have to stand up and be counted. There is too much at stake to let ten million black Christians continue to drift when we could see their potential energized in a tremendous way in the cause of Christ and world evangelism.

CHAPTER TWENTY-ONE

Once Around Jericho

Now let me say something to my black brother.

Obviously there is not going to be any real change if we expect only the white Christian to make all the efforts necessary. There is much we can do and should do and must do if we are going to realize the potential in our black churches.

I think we have to change our attitudes. We must come to the full realization that when God is black, God is *God*. He can do the same mighty exploits through us that He can through anyone else.

In this light we must stop feeling sorry for our black skin which brings injustice and discrimination. Isn't God bigger than these? If He can feed a multitude, heal the sick, raise the dead, overcome the devil himself, do you think for a moment that He can't overcome any apparent disadvantages of our blackness and all it represents?

So our black skin brings us lower paying jobs, poorer housing, inferior education for our children. Jesus suffered worse than these, yet He changed the course of the history of the world.

And this same Jesus lives in us.

We are going to have to change our attitudes about our responsibility to the world about us. We have been discriminated against and the white man owes us a lot in the secular sense. But as born again children of God we owe Him a lot, too.

The time has come for us to stop using the excuses that we can't go to the white Bible school or to the white conference grounds or go out as missionaries with white societies or join other white evangelical organizations, or even attend a white church if that is the place where you can get the best training to serve Jesus. If these institutions are the places we must go to be fully equipped for the work of the ministry then we must knock on their doors until they let us in. The tide of history is on our side. They are going to have to let us in, but we're going to have to do the knocking. We can't all wait until some enlightened white Christian comes to our door with a big scholarship and begs us to attend his school. The responsibility is ours just as much as it is his.

Man, take a look at my life again. Sure, I can sing and I learned to preach. But you have some abilities and talents I don't have. Look at Romans 12, and I Corinthians 12, and Ephesians 4 and you'll find that God has given gifts to *all* His people.

I had to fight — and I didn't always win — to have the chance to use my gifts and you probably will too. One school wouldn't take me and another wouldn't let me preach in their denomination. Finally they said I could preach but I couldn't become an ordained minister. I quit fighting for a while, but God opened some doors so that I could get after them again. Now, as a direct result of that fight, a black can go to any of their schools. I was their first ordained minister but they now have twenty-five and are begging for more. A few years ago they were ignoring blacks but now they are meeting frequently to talk about nothing but what they can do to help us get the training and challenge and experience we need to make something of ourselves.

Those first years as pastor in Fillmore were no cup of tea either. But I did the best I could in the situation where God put me, and it wasn't long before I was singing and preaching in Europe and Africa and Asia and Latin America. Then God opened up doors with Billy Graham and Overseas Crusades and formerly lily-white pulpits in conference centers and churches and schools.

God might not have the same program for you. The point is that He can and wants to develop your abilities to the very highest for His glory. If you're willing to take a chance and pay the price He'll do just that.

I'm not promising, of course, that everyone is going to make us feel entirely welcome and comfortable. But the Father didn't promise that to the Son when He sent Him into the world either. We are followers of Jesus first and blacks second or third or fourth.

And I'm not promising that some big white daddy is going to pay all the bills. Our young people are going to have to sweat and sacrifice and work and borrow to attend the camps and schools that are going to prepare us for service. Our pastors and our churches are going to have to raise scholarship funds and raise support for a host of black missionaries going out to the corners of the world.

I know our people will respond to the challenges of our day if some will just take the leadership. Rev. Ernie Johnson, then with Overseas Crusades, and I held a capsule missionary conference in the San Francisco Revival Center not too long ago. Rev. Don Green, pastor of the 250 members, realized that his black congregation knew little about missions but wanted to do something about it.

We started with a Friday night rally, held a men's breakast Saturday morning and a ladies' luncheon Saturday noon, and then emphasized missions in all departments and the church service on Sunday. It was thrilling to see the response. They had stretched their faith and set a goal to raise $5,000 for foreign missions. When their faith promises were counted, they had raised over $8,000.

One 65-year-old member said that he thought that missions was just for women. "At the men's breakfast I realized it was for men, too," he said as he made his faith promise. The whole congregation was turned on by the opportunities of service and involvement in foreign missions. The church pledged $100.00 a month to my ministry, promised to fully support a black missionary nurse to Haiti, and plans to send their pastor on a missionary tour.

Pastor Green's church is not a special case. The congregation consists of many domestics and others getting by on minimum salaries. But when the needs and opportunities and challenges of foreign missions were presented, they couldn't wait to get involved.

We need to see hundreds upon hundreds of missionary conferences like this in our churches across the land. You may have to join with a white church the first time to learn what to do and to get some of your top leaders enthused, but it will be well worth the effort.

I think the time is coming when we blacks are going to have to start our own black Christian institutions. I've been saying, for instance, that it is becoming more and more of an advantage to have a dark skin when going to the emerging nations of the world as missionaries.

But get this picture: You go to a country as a missionary. You convince the nationals that God is God of the brown man, too. Then the head of your mission visits the field. The man who makes the decisions, who handles the purse strings. His skin is white. Now what are you going to tell your nationals?

It was my pleasure to help start and serve as a board member for the Fellowship Bible Institute in San Francisco which now after ten years of operation has about fifty students. Dessy Webster, the founder and president, found an old house which he had rebuilt to serve as a school.

We need a lot of Dessy Websters who have vision and faith enough to start with whatever they have available.

There is much more we must do. I hope I've said much of this by my life and my testimony and hope you've gotten the picture. Now that you've read this book, go out and *do* something. Go out and *be* something. God *is* black, and God is *God*.

As I write this final chapter I feel a deep sense of guilt and frustration. In this last word I've been addressing my remarks to "white Christians" and to "black Christians" and thereby perpetrating the very idea I abhor.

In Jesus Christ we are not two groups but one.

Paul speaks of Christ's followers as making up a body.

This body of Jesus Christ is made up of black parts and white parts and brown parts and red parts and yellow parts. The white parts of the body of Christ cannot say to the black part, "You are only black, I have no need of you." Neither can the black part say, "Since I am only black, I don't have to take my responsibility in the body of Christ."

This cannot be any more than the eye can say to the hand, "I have no need of you," or the head to the feet, "I have no need of you" (I Cor. 12:21).

In this book I have had to refer to "white Christians" and "black Christians" simply as a practical matter to be understood. But my dream and my prayer is that someday we will be able to say these words about "black" and "white" Christians:

> On the contrary, the parts of the body which seem to be weaker are indispensable, and those parts of the body which we think less honorable we invest with the greater honor, and our unpresentable parts are treated with greater modesty, which our more presentable parts do not require. But God has so adjusted the body, giving the greater honor to the inferior part, that there may be no discord in the body, but that the members may have the same care for one another. If one member suffers, all suffer together; if one member is honored, all rejoice together.
> Now you [black, brown, white] are the body of Christ. . . . (I Cor. 12:22-27 R.S.V.).

When Christians everywhere finally realize that we are one body, we won't have to talk anymore about what happens when God is black. All of us will coordinate together as one beautiful body, each having the opportunity and accepting the responsibility for going into all the world and preaching the Gospel to every creature.

The walls have come tumblin' down in my life, but for the whole black church we've only been once around Jericho. We have twelve more laps and a great shout to go before the enemy is defeated.

May Christians of all colors join together to bring the victory. For the enemy is not the white man or the black man but the devil himself. Let us together be more than conquerors for Christ.

"Oh, God, Mankind is so sick and helpless to find a
remedy for the sickness.
And those who try to cure, who even suffer for their
fellow man, receive destruction.
Envies and spite are handed out instead of understanding.
Suffering is paid with cruelty, love with hate.
How many days of sadness must we spend to turn
hatred into gladness?

Please, God, how much sorrow must we spend to get
a future for tomorrow?
This world used to mean so very much.
Why did it change man's happiness to misery and heart-
break?
Why must we be lonely?
Is it sin and evil in our hearts?
What must we do?

Dear God of love, forgive, forgive.
  Teach us truly how to live.
Ask us not our race or creed.
  Just take us in our hour of need.
And let us know You love us, too.
  And that we are a part of You.
And someday may man realize,
  That all the earth, the seas, the skies,
Belong to God who made us all:
  The rich, the poor, the great, the small.
And in the Father's holy sight,
  No man is yellow, black or white.
And peace on earth cannot be found
  Until we meet on common ground.
And every man becomes a brother
  Who truly worships God and really loves each other."

(Original prayer of Bob Harrison on 45 RPM Record)